Ross Dobson

3 ways with...

MURDOCH BOOKS

contents

a few of my favourite things... 6

how it works... 8

the 100 ingredients 9

ingredients from...

the fridge 10

the freezer 58

the pantry 84

recipe index 216

a few of my favourite things...

Raindrops on roses and whiskers on kittens are not on my list of favourite things — or that is, not when it comes to stocking the fridge and pantry. Instead, my list is full of basic, readily available ingredients that have multiple uses and have the added benefit of making my cooking life easier.

Let's face it — we all have our favourites. I have a top ten which keeps changing — depending on my mood or the season — but will almost always include tinned tomatoes and barbecued chickens. Anchovies and curry pastes. Coconut milk and feta. Dried pasta and instant polenta. Tofu and soy sauce.

And bread. Stale, of course. It isn't the best word to associate with food but let's face it, 'stale' is what happens to bread. And due to one of life's more unfortunate paradoxes, the better the bread, the quicker it stales. But don't worry — fresh bread doesn't make for good crumbing!

Your kitchen is probably already filled with many of the 100 ingredients featured in this book (they've all been in my top 10 at some time). I make no attempt to reinvent your pantry or prescribe what you *should* have in your kitchen. Instead, I'm offering you *3 ways with...* those ingredients you'll already have to hand. These base ingredients are here to act as a framework for the start of something good.

Whatever I cook I want there to be a little magic involved. A little 'I can't believe I made this'. Simplicity is the key here.

For the recipes with a short cooking time, you only want to whiz, chop, toss, fry or boil a few ingredients to make something delicious. Take the creamy artichoke soup recipe (page 91). It has four ingredients. Heat in a saucepan. Whiz in a food processor. Ready in 15 minutes. Or the white bean and tuna salad (page 103). Open a tin. Chop and toss together. Ready in 10 minutes. Done deal.

For me, it's also okay for recipes to have a long cooking time — just as long as they have next to no prep time! So don't be afraid when you see the words 'slow' and 'cooking' used together. Slow cooking is like alchemy. It's even more magical when you can prepare it quickly and leave it to do its own thing.

The important thing is don't fuss too much and you will enjoy it even more. Like the recipe for slow-cooked lamb shanks with lentils (page 131). It's actually scary how short this recipe is. It has a handful of ingredients and about 10 seconds prep time (you have to chop some pancetta). Actually, make that 20 seconds prep time (you also have to open a tin of tomatoes). Put it all in a pot for a couple of hours. Take a bath. Do a yoga class. Walk the dog. Lift the lid and voila! You won't believe you made it. This is the magic I'm talking about.

What are your favourite things? I hope you find many of them in them in the 300 recipes in this book. You don't need pictures to inspire you. Have a look in your fridge, freezer or pantry. The inspiration is there already.

Enjoy!

how it works...

The recipes in *3 ways with...* don't look like other recipes. There are no long, complicated recipes. The recipes have a casual, relaxed feel — a handful of this, a squeeze of that. Each recipe serves 4 (unless it says otherwise). The recipes don't get bogged down in detail — so neither should you.

ten steps for *3 ways with...*

1   Choose an ingredient from the list of 100 (see the next page).

2   Go to the page you need and read the three ways you have to use that ingredient.

3   Choose a recipe you like. Or...

4   ... if you are cooking for others call, email or send them a text message with their 3 options (believe me, they will be impressed at your knowledge, versatility and cooking skills).

5   Make a shopping list. This is made easy. The highlighted words in the text are the ingredients you'll need.

6   Do a quick shop — in your lunch break or on your way home. Or...

7   ... since some of the recipes are so simple, find the ingredients at home.

8   Before cooking, read the recipe again and check out all those things which make cooking easy, casual and relaxed. Things like making sure you know the cooking time, having the oven hot and ready to go, having the prepared ingredients at hand.

9   Always keep the book somewhere obvious so others can see how great it is. Or...

10 ... if you want people to believe you are a naturally versatile and really talented cook, hide this book.

the 100 ingredients

almonds 87
anchovies 89
artichokes 91
bacon 13
balsamic vinegar 93
barbecued chicken 15
bean thread noodles 95
beer 17
berries 61
black olives 19
blue cheese 21
broad beans 63
buckwheat noodles 97
burritos and tortillas 99
butterbeans 101
cannellini beans 103
capers 105
cashews 107
cheddar 23
chicken stock 109
chickpeas 111
chocolate 113
chorizo 25
coconut milk 115
corn 65
couscous 117
cream cheese 27
curry powder 119
desiccated coconut 121
dried apricots 123
dried mushrooms 125
egg noodles 29
feta 31
filo 67

firm tofu 33
fish sauce 127
green curry paste 129
green lentils 131
green olives 35
ham 37
hoisin sauce 133
honey 135
hot pepper sauce 137
ice cream 69
indian curry paste 139
jam 141
kidney beans 143
lasagne sheets 39
lime pickle 145
long-grain rice 147
long pasta 149
madeira cake 151
maple syrup 153
marmalade 155
mascarpone 41
mayonnaise 43
meringues 157
miso 159
mozzarella 45
mustard 161
oats 163
oyster sauce 165
panettone 167
parmesan 47
peanuts 169
peanut butter 171
peas 71

pine nuts 173
polenta 175
pizza bases 73
prawns 75
puff pastry 77
red and brown lentils 177
red curry paste 179
red wine 181
red wine vinegar 183
rice wine 185
ricotta 49
salmon 187
sesame seeds 189
shortcrust pastry 79
short-grain rice 191
short pasta 193
soft tofu 51
sour cream 53
soy sauce 195
spinach 81
stale bread 197
sweet chilli sauce 199
tahini 201
tomatoes 203
tomato passata 205
tuna 207
turkish bread 209
udon noodles 211
vine leaves 83
walnuts 213
white vinegar 215
white wine 55
yoghurt 57

9

3 ways with...

ingredients from the fridge

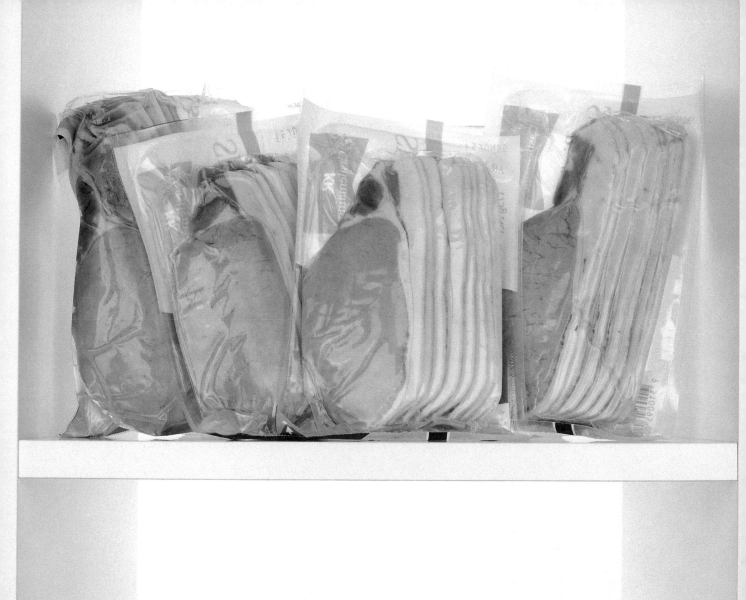

bacon is also used in recipes on pages...
27, 53, 109, 137 and 181.

bacon

three ways with

penne with bacon, chilli and tomato

Cook 400 g (14 oz) **penne** in boiling water for 8–10 minutes. Drain and return to the pan. Meanwhile, heat a splash of **olive oil** in a frying pan, add 4 chopped **bacon slices** and stir-fry over a high heat for a few minutes, so the bacon sizzles and crisps and flavours the oil. Add 1 chopped **onion**, 2 chopped **garlic cloves**, 2 seeded and chopped **small red chillies** and stir-fry for a few minutes, to soften the onion. Add 400 g (14 oz) tinned **chopped tomatoes** and 125 ml (4 fl oz/ 1/2 cup) water to the pan. Bring the sauce to the boil then simmer for 10 minutes. Add the sauce to the pasta and stir to coat the pasta over a low heat for a minute to warm through. Serve with grated **parmesan**.

egg and bacon pie

Have your oven hot and ready at 220°C (425°F/Gas 7). Line a 1.5 litre (52 fl oz/6 cup) baking dish with frozen **puff pastry** and cook in the oven for 10 minutes. Cook 6–8 roughly chopped **bacon slices** in a non-stick frying pan for 5 minutes, stirring over a medium heat. Allow to cool. Place half the bacon over the baked pastry. Carefully break 8 **eggs** on top of the bacon and lightly season. Add 2 tablespoons chopped **flat-leaf (Italian) parsley** on top of the eggs and top with the remaining bacon. Bake for 20–25 minutes, until the eggs are cooked and the pastry golden. Great for winter supper with **potato mash**.

warm spinach, egg and bacon salad

Place 3–4 large handfuls **baby English spinach leaves** and 3 roughly chopped **hard-boiled eggs** in a large bowl. Heat a few splashes of **light olive oil** in a frying pan and cook 3 roughly chopped **bacon slices** for 4–5 minutes, just so the bacon starts to turn golden and crispy. Remove the pan from the heat and add 1 crushed **garlic clove**, 1 teaspoon **mild mustard** and 1 tablespoon **red wine** to the hot bacon, stirring quickly to combine. Pour all the ingredients, including the hot oil from the pan, over the spinach. Toss together, so the spinach just begins to wilt, and add some **black pepper** to serve.

barbecued chicken is also used in recipes on pages...
43, 109, 189, 199, 201 and 213.

barbecued chicken

three ways with

chicken and vegetable pot pie

Have your oven hot and ready at 220°C (425°F/Gas 7). Heat 60 g (2¼ oz) **butter** in a frying pan. When sizzling hot, add 1 chopped **carrot** and 2 chopped **celery stalks** and stir-fry for a few minutes. Add 2 tablespoons **plain (all-purpose) flour** and cook for 2 minutes (it should thickly coat the vegetables, but be careful not to burn the flour). Add the chopped meat from half a **barbecued chicken**, 80 g (2¾ oz/½ cup) **peas** and a handful of chopped **flat-leaf (Italian) parsley**. Stir around for a minute then add 500 ml (17 fl oz/2 cups) **chicken stock** and 250 ml (9 fl oz/1 cup) **pouring (whipping) cream**. Season well and slowly bring to the boil, stirring constantly, until slightly thickened. Spoon into an ovenproof dish and top with some **puff pastry**, trimmed to fit the dish, or a layer of **potato mash** and bake for 20–25 minutes, until the pastry is golden.

tex-mex chicken salad

Mash 1 **avocado** in a bowl with 125 g (4½ oz/½ cup) **sour cream** and 2 tablespoons **lemon juice** and season well. Put the shredded meat and skin of a **barbecued chicken** in a bowl with 1 **red onion** sliced into thin wedges, 2 **large tomatoes**, chopped into bite-sized pieces, 1 handful **pitted black olives**, 1 large handful chopped **coriander (cilantro) leaves and stems**, 3 tablespoons **jalapeño chillies (in brine)** and 3–4 handfuls shredded **iceberg lettuce**. Toss to combine and top with dollops of the avocado dressing. Serve in warm **taco shells**.

chinatown chicken and watercress salad

Cut the meat and skin of a **barbecued chicken** into thin strips. Put in a bowl with 250 g (9 oz) halved **cherry tomatoes**, 1 large handful roughly chopped **coriander (cilantro) leaves**, 3 thinly sliced **spring onions (scallions)** and 200 g (7 oz) **watercress**, leaves picked. Toss gently to combine. Combine 2 tablespoons **light soy sauce**, 2 tablespoons **rice vinegar**, 1 teaspoon **sugar**, 1 teaspoon **sesame oil** and 1 teaspoon grated **ginger** in a bowl. Pour over the salad to serve.

barbecued chicken / fridge

beer

three ways with

steak, onion and ale casserole

Have your oven hot and ready at 160°C (315°F/Gas 2–3). Chop 1 kg (2 lb 4 oz) **chuck** or **stewing steak** into large bite-sized pieces and toss around in a bowl with 60 g (2¼ oz/½ cup) **plain (all-purpose) flour**, 1 teaspoon **sea salt** and ½ teaspoon **white pepper**. Heat a splash of **olive oil** and 40 g (1½ oz) **butter** in a large ovenproof saucepan and cook the beef in 2 batches for 2–3 minutes, to gently sizzle and turn brown. Put the browned beef in a bowl. Add 4 peeled and quartered **onions** to the pan and cook for 8–10 minutes, stirring often, so the onions soften and turn golden. Return the beef to the pan with 350 ml (12 fl oz) **ale** or **beer**, 1 litre (35 fl oz/4 cups) **beef stock** and 2 **bay leaves**. Boil, stirring once or twice, then cover with a piece of crumpled baking paper and cook in the oven for 2 hours. Remove and cook on a rapid simmer for 20 minutes, so the sauce is thick and glossy. Serve with **potato mash**.

slow braised lamb shank and vegetable hotpot

Have your oven hot and ready at 160°C (315°F/Gas 2–3). Heat a splash of **olive oil** in a casserole dish and cook 1 chopped **onion** and 2 chopped **garlic cloves** in the oil for 2–3 minutes, so the onion gently softens and sizzles. Add 375 ml (13 fl oz/1½ cups) **beer**, 250 ml (9 fl oz/1 cup) **chicken stock** and a splash of **worcestershire sauce** to the pan and bring to the boil. Add 4 trimmed **lamb shanks**, place a tight-fitting lid on the dish and cook in the oven for 1½ hours. Remove from the oven and turn the lamb shanks, basting in the gravy. Add 2 peeled and quartered **large potatoes** and 2 chopped **carrots**, season well and return to the oven for 1 hour. Stir through a handful of roughly chopped **flat-leaf (Italian) parsley** and serve.

sweet and sour tapas chorizo

Stir-fry 1 finely chopped **red onion** in 1 tablespoon **olive oil** for a few minutes, so the onion sizzles and softens. Add 1 tablespoon **soft brown sugar** and 1 sliced **chorizo** and cook for 2–3 minutes, so the sausage slices start to brown. Add 400 g (14 oz) tinned **cannellini beans**, rinsed and drained, 125 ml (4 fl oz/½ cup) **beer**, 3 tablespoons **red wine vinegar** and 1 **bay leaf** to the pan and boil for 6–8 minutes, until almost all the liquid has evaporated. Serve as a shared starter with warm **bread**.

black olives are also used in recipes on pages...
15, 31, 43, 55, 101, 103, 105, 161, 181, 191, 207 and 209.

black olives

three ways with

herby olive sauce

Blend 185 g (6 1/2 oz/1 1/2 cups) pitted black olives, 1 small handful each flat-leaf (Italian) parsley and basil, 1 tablespoon oregano and a good squeeze of lemon juice in a food processor until you have a chunky paste. With the motor running, slowly pour in 3 tablespoons good fruity olive oil. Keep in a bowl and taste for seasoning. Serve with chargrilled octopus or spoon onto barbecued lamb cutlets.

olive and roasted cherry tomato pasta sauce

Have your oven hot and ready at 180°C (350°F/Gas 4). Put 500 g (1 lb 2 oz) cherry tomatoes in a bowl with 3 tablespoons light olive oil, 2 chopped garlic cloves, 1 bay leaf, 2 teaspoons oregano, 1 teaspoon sea salt and a pinch of sugar. Toss around in the bowl a few times and put all the ingredients on a baking tray and cook in the oven for 30 minutes. Remove from the oven and allow to cool on the tray for the flavours to intensify. Cook 400 g (14 oz) of your favourite pasta (long varieties go well with this sauce). Put the tomatoes in a saucepan with 60 g (2 1/4 oz/1/2 cup) pitted black olives and heat through. Spoon the sauce over the pasta and serve with grated parmesan.

penne with olives, tuna and chilli herbs

Cook 400 g (14 oz) penne in boiling water for 8–10 minutes. Drain and return to the warm pan. Meanwhile, cook 1 sliced red onion, 2 seeded and chopped small red chillies and 2 chopped garlic cloves in 3 tablespoons light olive oil for 4–5 minutes, so the onion gently sizzles and softens in the oil. Add 185 g (6 1/2 oz) tinned tuna to the pan with a handful each chopped basil, mint and flat-leaf (Italian) parsley and stir around over a gentle heat to warm the tuna through, but not breaking up too much. Add to the pasta and gently heat for 2–3 minutes. Season well and serve.

blue cheese is also used in recipes on pages...
41 and 91.

blue cheese

three ways with

blue cheese and broad bean risotto

Simmer 750 ml (26 fl oz/3 cups) chicken stock. Cook 1 chopped small onion and 1 chopped garlic clove in a splash of olive oil, so the onion gently sizzles and softens and turns opaque. Add 110 g (3³/4 oz/¹/2 cup) arborio or risotto rice, stir for 1 minute then add 125 ml (4 fl oz/¹/2 cup) of the stock to the saucepan, stirring until the rice has absorbed almost all the liquid. Repeat until all the stock is in the pan and the rice is soft but has a little bite in the centre. Stir through 3 tablespoons crumbled blue cheese, 20 g (³/4 oz) butter and 95 g (3¹/4 oz/ ¹/2 cup) blanched and peeled broad beans. Season well and serve this rich risotto as a starter.

blue cheese and peach salad

Put 1 bunch frisée, washed and trimmed (or 3–4 large handfuls of mixed salad leaf) in a large bowl. In a small bowl combine 2 teaspoons sherry vinegar or white wine vinegar, 2 tablespoons olive oil, 1 teaspoon dijon mustard and black pepper. Add 2–3 sliced peaches to the salad, pour over the dressing and toss to combine. Top the salad with 3 tablespoons crumbled blue cheese and serve.

blue cheese and walnut pizza with pear and rocket salad

Have your oven hot and ready at 200°C (400°F/Gas 6). Place a frozen pizza base on a baking tray and into the oven for 10 minutes. Remove, brush with a little olive oil and top each pizza with 150 g (5¹/2 oz/1 cup) crumbled blue cheese and 125 g (4¹/2 oz/1 cup) roughly chopped walnuts. Return to the oven for about 8 minutes, so the cheese is gooey and the walnuts are slightly golden. Remove the pizza and top with 2 handfuls baby rocket (arugula) leaves, half a sliced firm brown pear, a good grinding of black pepper and a drizzling of olive oil. Cut into wedges and serve. Serves 2.

cheddar is also used in recipes on pages...
37, 143 and 187.

cheddar

three ways with

chicken and leek pasta

Cook 400 g (14 oz) **small shell pasta** in boiling water for 8–10 minutes. Drain well and return to the saucepan. Heat 60 g (2¼ oz) **butter** in a saucepan. When the butter sizzles, add 1 finely sliced **leek** and stir-fry for a few minutes, until soft and silky. Add 2 cubed **boneless, skinless chicken breasts** and stir-fry for 5 minutes, so the chicken starts to turn golden. Add 2 tablespoons **plain (all-purpose) flour** and cook for 1 minute, stirring constantly (it should look like a thick paste coating the leeks) and gradually pour in 500 ml (17 fl oz/2 cups) **milk**. Cook on a gentle heat, stirring constantly, until thick and smooth. Add 125 g (4½ oz/1 cup) grated **cheddar**, 50 g (1¾ oz/½ cup) grated **parmesan** and stir until the cheese has melted. Stir through the pasta and spoon into a large serving dish. Sprinkle with more **cheddar** and **parmesan** and cook under a hot grill (broiler) until the top is golden and crisp.

really cheesy cauliflower

Have your oven hot and ready at 180°C (350°F/Gas 4). Break 8 large pieces off a head of **cauliflower** and cook in boiling water for 5 minutes. Drain and place the pieces to fit snugly in a baking dish. Put 250 ml (9 fl oz/1 cup) **pouring (whipping) cream**, 1 tablespoon **plain (all-purpose) flour** and 2 teaspoons **mild mustard** in a saucepan and gently heat, stirring constantly until smooth. Add 125 g (4½ oz/1 cup) grated **cheddar** to the pan, stir around until the cheese has just melted then pour over the cauliflower pieces. Sprinkle 60 g (2¼ oz/½ cup) extra grated **cheddar** on top and bake for 30 minutes.

tuna casserole

Have your oven hot and ready at 180°C (350°F/Gas 4). Combine 370 g (13 oz) tinned **tuna**, drained of excess oil, 250 g (9 oz/1 cup) **sour cream**, 125 g (4½ oz/1 cup) grated **cheddar**, 125 ml (4 fl oz/½ cup) **milk**, 1 tablespoon **cornflour (cornstarch)** and 3 chopped **spring onions (scallions)** in a bowl. Spoon into a 1.5 litre (52 fl oz/6 cup) ceramic baking dish, top with 60 g (4½ oz/½ cup) grated **cheddar**, sprinkle with **paprika** and cook in the oven for 40 minutes.

cheddar / fridge

chorizo is also used in recipes on pages...
17, 111 and 131.

chorizo

three ways with

paprika risoni hotpot

Cook 1 chopped **red onion**,
1 chopped **garlic clove** and
1 chopped **chorizo** in a splash of
olive oil for 5 minutes, so the
onion sizzles in the oil and to
release all the hidden spices in the
sausage. Add 1/2 teaspoon **smoked
paprika** and 200 g (7 oz/1 cup)
risoni, and stir to coat the risoni
in the spicy pan juices. Add 400 g
(14 oz) tinned **chopped tomatoes**
and 500 ml (17 fl oz/2 cups)
chicken stock and bring to the
boil. Place on a tight-fitting lid
and cook over a very low heat for
20 minutes. Remove from the heat
and leave the lid on for a further
5 minutes. Remove, stir through
a handful of chopped **flat-leaf
(Italian) parsley**, and serve hot.

spanish minestrone

Heat a generous splash of **olive
oil** in a saucepan and stir-fry
1 chopped **onion** with 1 finely
cubed **chorizo** for 4–5 minutes
on a medium heat, to soften the
onion and bring out all the spices
in the sausage. Add 500 ml
(17 fl oz/2 cups) **chicken stock**,
400 g (14 oz) tinned **chopped
tomatoes**, 400 g (14 oz) tinned
cannellini beans, rinsed and
drained, and 1 finely cubed **potato**.
Bring to the boil and simmer for
15 minutes, until the potato is
nicely soft. Stir through a handful
of roughly chopped **flat-leaf
(Italian) parsley** and serve topped
with some crumbled **feta** or
manchego cheese.

chorizo and seafood gumbo

Cook 12 **raw prawns (shrimp)**
in a splash of **light olive oil** for
2 minutes each side, so they turn
pink and flavour the oil. Remove
from the pan. Add 1 chopped
chorizo, 1 chopped **onion**, 1 small
cubed **green capsicum (pepper)**,
2 sliced **celery stalks** and
1/2 teaspoon each **cayenne pepper**
and **black pepper** to the pan and
cook for 5 minutes. Add 1 litre
(35 fl oz/4 cups) **chicken stock**
and 3 tablespoons **medium-grain
rice** and boil for 20–25 minutes,
so the rice is really soft. Return
the prawns to the pan with 300 g
(10 1/2 oz) bite-sized cubes of **white
fish fillet** and 12 **mussels**. Stir
around to coat the seafood in
the gumbo, cover and simmer for
10 minutes, so the fish turns white
and the mussels open. Serve in
large bowls.

cream cheese

three ways with

creamy potato and leek soup

Cook 2 sliced **leeks** in 40 g (1¹/₂ oz) gently sizzling **butter** for a few minutes, until soft and silky. Add 2 litres (70 fl oz/8 cups) **chicken stock**, 2 peeled and cubed **large all-purpose potatoes** and cook on a rapid simmer for 10 minutes, so the potatoes soften but don't break up. Reduce the heat to really low and stir through 125 g (4¹/₂ oz/ ¹/₂ cup) **cream cheese**, a handful of finely chopped **flat-leaf (Italian) parsley**, a tablespoon of snipped **chives** and some **black pepper**. Cook on a gentle heat for a few more minutes. Serve with **buttered toast** on the side.

fettucine boscaiola

Cook 2 **bacon slices** and 1 chopped **onion** in a small splash of **olive oil** for 4–5 minutes. Add 180 g (6¹/₂ oz/2 cups) sliced **button mushrooms** and 1 chopped **garlic clove** and stir-fry for 2–3 minutes, to soften the mushrooms. Chop a 300 g (10¹/₂ oz) block of **cream cheese** into 8 cubes and add to the pan. Stir over a gentle heat until the cream cheese has melted evenly. Remove from the heat and cover to keep warm. Meanwhile, cook 400 g (14 oz) **fettucine** in boiling water for 8–10 minutes. Drain well and return to the warm pan with the sauce and 50 g (1³/₄ oz/¹/₂ cup) grated parmesan and a good grinding of **black pepper**. Stir to coat the pasta in the sauce. Top with extra **parmesan** and serve.

cream cheese and cherry danish

Have your oven hot and ready at 220°C (425°F/Gas 7). Line a baking tray with baking paper. Cut a sheet of **puff pastry** into four equal squares and place on the baking tray. Put a tablespoon of **cream cheese** in the centre of each square with a tablespoon of **cherry jam** (or your favourite) on top. Bring the four points of the pastry towards the centre and pinch or twist firmly. Don't worry if there are little gaps in the pastry. The cheese and jam will leak out and look gooey and yummy. Bake for 20 minutes, until puffed and golden. Allow to cool before lightly dusting with **icing (confectioners') sugar**. Serve with **coffee** for brunch, or hot with **ice cream** for dessert.

egg noodles

these ways with

yum cha noodles

Cook 300 g (10½ oz) **fresh Chinese egg noodles** in boiling water for 2 minutes (or 3–4 minutes if using dried). Rinse under cold water, drain really well and toss the noodles around in a bowl with 2 teaspoons **sesame oil**. Heat 2 tablespoons **vegetable oil** in a hot wok. Add 1 chopped **garlic clove**, 2 teaspoons grated **ginger**, 125 g (4½ oz/1 cup) **garlic chives**, cut into 3 cm (1¼ inch) lengths, and 180 g (6½ oz/2 cups) **bean sprouts** for a minute, just so the vegetables wilt. Add the noodles to the wok and stir-fry for 2–3 minutes. Add 2 tablespoons **light soy sauce** and 2 tablespoons **oyster sauce** to the wok and stir-fry for 2 minutes, ensuring all the noodles are evenly coated in the sauce. Serve spinkled with 1 tablespoon lightly toasted **sesame seeds**.

a short long soup

Cook 300 g (10½ oz) **fresh Chinese egg noodles** in boiling water for 2 minutes (or 3–4 minutes if using dried) and drain. Boil 1 litre (35 fl oz/4 cups) **chicken stock** with a splash of **light soy sauce** to season. Add 200 g (7 oz/1 cup) sliced **Chinese barbecued pork (char siu)** and 1 bunch roughly chopped **Chinese broccoli (gai larn)** to the pot and cook for 2 minutes, so the greens turn emerald and soften. Put the noodles into serving bowls and spoon over the hot soup mixture. Top with sliced **spring onions (scallions)** and a drizzling of **sesame oil**.

cold tossed noodle salad

Put 2 tablespoons **dried shrimp** (available from the Asian section at supermarkets) in a bowl and cover with boiling water for 10 minutes. Drain well and finely chop. Cook 300 g (10½ oz) **fresh Chinese egg noodles** in boiling water for 2 minutes (or 3–4 minutes if using dried) and drain. Combine 3 tablespoons **light soy sauce**, 2 tablespoons **rice vinegar**, 2 teaspoons finely grated **ginger**, 2 teaspoons **sesame oil** and a good pinch of **sugar** in a small bowl. Pour over the noodles and add the chopped shrimp. Toss around for a minute to really coat the noodles in the dressing. Finely slice a **small carrot**, a **small red capsicum (pepper)** and 4 **spring onions (scallions)** and add to the noodles with 1 large handful **coriander (cilantro) leaves**, roughly chopped, and toss well.

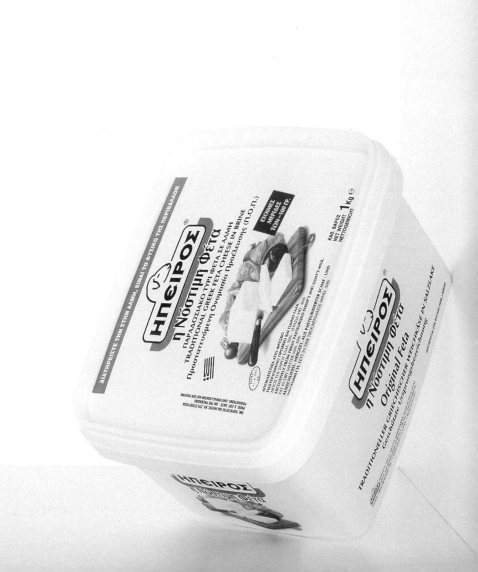

feta is also used in recipes on pages...
25, 63, 67, 91, 97, 99, 107, 123 and 131.

feta

three ways with

artichoke, orange and feta salad

Cut 6 tinned and drained **artichokes** in half and put in a bowl with 2 peeled and segmented **oranges**, 1 finely sliced **red onion**, 1 large handful each **flat-leaf (Italian) parsley** and **mint**, 140 g (5 oz/ 1 cup) cubed **marinated feta** and 80 g ($2^3/4$ oz/$^1/2$ cup) pitted **kalamata olives**. Combine 2 tablespoons good **olive oil** in a bowl with 1 tablespoon **red wine vinegar**, 1 crushed **garlic clove** and **salt** and **black pepper**. Pour the dressing over the salad and gently toss to combine. Serve with **grilled swordfish** or **tuna steaks**.

creamy feta salad dressing

Put 225 g (8 oz/$1^1/2$ cups) crumbled **feta** in a food processor with 2 crushed **garlic cloves**, 1 tablespoon chopped **dill** and 3 tablespoons **olive oil**. With the motor running, slowly add 185 ml (6 fl oz/$^3/4$ cup) **milk** in a steady stream to form a thick and smooth dressing. Serve dollops over **grilled lamb** or **vegetables**.

prawns with feta

Cut 4 ripe and tasty **tomatoes** in half, squeeze out as many seeds as you can and roughly chop. Heat 2–3 tablespoons of good **fruity olive oil** in a hot frying pan and add 1 chopped **onion** and 1 chopped **garlic clove**, stirring around for 2–3 minutes to soften the onion and flavour the oil. Add the tomatoes, 1 teaspoon **dried oregano** and a small handful of roughly chopped **flat-leaf (Italian) parsley** to the pan. Cook for 2–3 minutes so the tomatoes really sizzle. Add 16 peeled and deveined **raw prawns (shrimp)** to the pan and cook for 5 minutes, so the prawns turn pink and curly. Add 3 tablespoons water and boil for a few minutes. Stir through 150 g ($5^1/2$ oz/1 cup) roughly crumbled **feta** and serve as a meal with **rice** or as a shared tapas dish with **bread**.

USED BY:

660g Net

Keep refrigerated: 2°C - 7°C

- NO CHOLESTEROL
- HIGH IN PROTEIN
- PASTEURISED
- 不含膽固醇
- 含豐富蛋白質
- 高溫殺菌處理

Hard
Tofu
大豆干

Product of Australia
Manufactured and Packed by: Fortune Soy Manufacturer Pty Ltd.
111 Fairford Road Padstow N.S.W. 2211 Sydney Australia Ph:(02) 9771 1808 Fax:(02) 9773 9300

USED BY:

660g Net

Keep refrigerated: 2°C - 7°C

- NO CHOLESTEROL
- HIGH IN PROTEIN
- PASTEURISED
- 不含膽固醇
- 含豐富蛋白質
- 高溫殺菌處理

Hard
Tofu
大豆干

Product of Australia
Manufactured and Packed by: Fortune Soy Manufacturer Pty Ltd.
111 Fairford Road Padstow N.S.W. 2211 Sydney Australia Ph:(02) 9771 1808 Fax:(02) 9773

USED BY:

660g Net

Keep refrigerated: 2°C - 7°C

- NO CHOLESTEROL
- HIGH IN PROTEIN
- PASTEURISED
- 不含膽固醇
- 含豐富蛋白質
- 高溫殺菌處理

Hard
Tofu
大豆干

Product of Australia
Manufactured and Packed by: Fortune Soy Manufacturer Pty Ltd.
111 Fairford Road Padstow N.S.W. 2211 Sydney Australia Ph:(02) 9771 1808 Fax:(02) 9773 9300

USED BY:
Keep refrigerated: 2°C - 7°C

- NO CHOLESTEROL
- HIGH IN PROTEIN
- PASTEURISED
- 不含膽固醇
- 含豐富蛋白質
- 高溫殺菌處理

660g Net

Product of Australia
Manufactured and Packed by: Fortune Soy
Manufacturer Pty Ltd.
111 Fairford Road Padstow N.S.W. 2211 Sydney Australia Ph:(02) 9771 1808 Fax:(02) 9773 9300

Hard
Tofu
大豆干

firm tofu is also used in recipes on pages...
93, 125 and 195.

firm tofu

three ways with

tofu and zucchini omelette

Stir-fry 1 grated zucchini (courgette) in a splash of vegetable oil in a non-stick frying pan for 2–3 minutes. Add 2 handfuls baby English spinach leaves and a few splashes of light soy sauce to the pan cook for 2–3 minutes, so the spinach wilts. Put 185 g (6¹/2 oz/ 1 cup) cubed firm tofu over the spinach. Beat 3 eggs and pour into the pan and cook on a high heat for 2–3 minutes, so the edges start to puff up. Place under a hot grill (broiler) until golden and firm. Serve the omelette topped with a drizzle of oyster sauce and some white pepper. Serves 2.

chinatown mushroom and tofu stir-fry

Cut a 300 g (10¹/2 oz) block of firm tofu into 16 small pieces. Have a wok hot and ready to go. Add 125 ml (4 fl oz/¹/2 cup) light cooking oil to the wok. When the oil is shimmering, add the tofu pieces and fry for 3–4 minutes, until just starting to turn golden. Leaving the tofu, drain all but a tablespoon of oil from the wok. Add 2 sliced spring onions (scallions) and 2 teaspoons grated ginger and stir-fry for a few seconds, then add 500 g (1 lb 2 oz) mixed Asian mushrooms (try shiitake, shimeji, oyster, enoki and maybe even some swiss browns, all ends trimmed off if need be) and stir-fry for 3–4 minutes. Just when the mushrooms turn limp, add 3 tablespoons oyster sauce and 1 tablespoon soy sauce. Stir-fry to coat all the ingredients in the sauce and serve.

braised tofu in ginger, spring onion and oyster sauce

Cut a 600 g (1 lb 5 oz) block of firm tofu into 3 cm (1¹/4 inch) cubes and place on paper towel. Heat 250 ml (9 fl oz/1 cup) vegetable oil in a wok. Cook half the tofu pieces in the hot oil for 5–6 minutes, turning often, so they sizzle and become golden. Remove to a plate, then cook the remaining tofu. Drain the oil from the wok. Return all the tofu to the wok with 250 ml (9 fl oz/ 1 cup) chicken stock, 2 tablespoons oyster sauce, 2 teaspoons cornflour (cornstarch), 4–6 thin slices of ginger, 1 chopped garlic clove and 4 spring onions (scallions), chopped into 4 cm (1¹/2 inch) lengths, and bring to the boil, stirring constantly. Turn the tofu pieces over in the thickened sauce, cook for 2 minutes and serve with rice.

green olives are also used in recipes on pages...
183 and 207.

green olives

three ways with

roasted chicken with green olives, balsamic and capers

Have your oven hot and ready at 180°C (350°F/Gas 4). Season 4 **chicken legs and thighs** with **sea salt** and **black pepper**. Heat 3 tablespoons **light olive oil** in a heavy-based frying pan. Cook half the chicken in the hot oil for 3–4 minutes each side, so the pieces are golden and the skin looks crispy. Repeat with the remaining chicken and place all the chicken in a flat baking dish. Pour 125 ml (4 fl oz/^{1}/$_2$ cup) **balsamic vinegar** over the chicken pieces and add 175 g (6 oz/1 cup) **green olives** and 1 tablespoon rinsed **baby capers**. Cook in the oven for 1 hour, turning the chicken every 20 minutes. Serve with a handful of chopped **flat-leaf (Italian) parsley** and 3 tablespoons lightly toasted **flaked almonds**. Serve with crispy **roast potatoes**.

orange and olive salad

Whisk together 125 g (4^1/$_2$ oz/ ^{1}/$_2$ cup) good **mayonnaise** with 2 tablespoons **sherry vinegar** (or any light vinegar) and 2 teaspoons finely chopped **tarragon**. Arrange 1 roughly chopped **cos (romaine) lettuce** on a plate and top with 2 peeled and finely sliced **oranges**, 1 finely sliced **red onion**, 175 g (6 oz/ 1 cup) **green olives**, 2 tablespoons rinsed **capers** and 6–8 **anchovy fillets**. Pour the dressing over the salad and serve as a starter or side to a main.

turkish olive and walnut salad

Pit and halve 350 g (12 oz/2 cups) **green olives** and toss the olives around in a bowl with 125 g (4^1/$_2$ oz/1 cup) roughly chopped **walnuts**, 1 finely sliced **red onion** and a large handful of chopped **flat-leaf (Italian) parsley**. Mix together 3 tablespoons good **fruity olive oil**, 1 tablespoon **balsamic vinegar**, ^{1}/$_2$ teaspoon **chilli flakes** and ^{1}/$_2$ teaspoon **caster (superfine) sugar**. Pour over the salad and toss once more. This salad is great with **spicy lamb meatballs**, **hummus** and warm Middle Eastern flat breads.

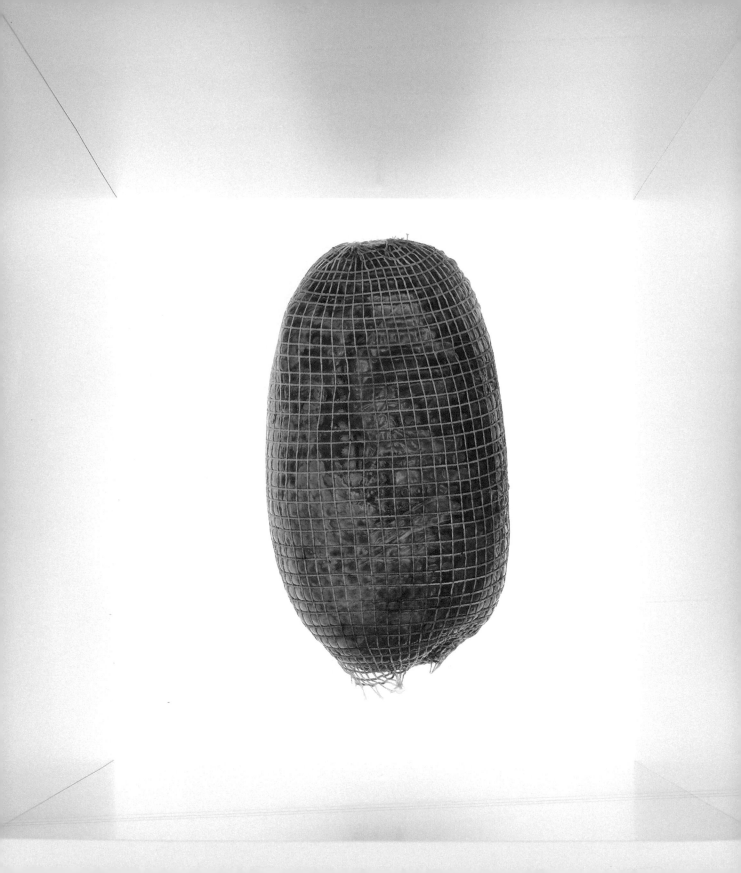

ham is also used in recipes on pages...
147 and 209.

ham

three ways with

baked macaroni cheese with ham

Have your oven hot and ready at 180°C (350°F/Gas 4). Cook 400 g (14 oz) **macaroni** in boiling water for 8–10 minutes. Drain and return to the pan. Heat 40 g (1¹/₂ oz) **butter** in a saucepan until it sizzles then stir in 2 tablespoons **plain (all-purpose) flour** over a low heat for 1 minute, until you have a smooth paste. Slowly add 500 ml (17 fl oz/2 cups) **milk** to the pan. You can turn the heat up here, but don't let the milk boil. Stir until you have a smooth sauce, a bit like thin custard. Add 60 g (2¹/₄ oz/¹/₂ cup) grated **cheddar** and 75 g (2¹/₂ oz/¹/₂ cup) grated **mozzarella** and stir over a low heat until the cheese has melted smoothly. Add the cheese sauce to the cooked macaroni with 155 g (5¹/₂ oz/1 cup) finely sliced **ham** then stir around and pour into a large ceramic baking dish. Sprinkle with 60 g (2¹/₄ oz/¹/₂ cup) grated **cheddar** and cook in the oven for 25–30 minutes, until golden on top.

croque madame

Sandwich some sliced **ham** between 2 slices of **buttered white bread** which has been smeared with a **mild mustard**. Heat a little **butter** in a non-stick frying pan and cook the sandwich for 2 minutes each side, until nicely golden. Place some thinly sliced **tasty cheese** on top (try an aged cheddar or tasty gruyère) and place under the grill (broiler) until the cheese is bubbly and golden. Fry an **egg**, sunny side up, in some good **olive oil** and slide the egg on top of the croque. Enjoy for brunch or supper. Serves 1.

ham, mushroom and mozzarella pizza

Have your oven hot and ready at 220°C (425°F/Gas 7). Place a baking tray (or better yet, a pizza stone) in the oven to really heat up. Defrost a frozen **pizza base** and evenly spread with 3 tablespoons **tomato passata (puréed tomatoes)**. Top with 155 g (5¹/₂ oz/1 cup) sliced **ham**, 90 g (3¹/₄ oz/1 cup) thinly sliced **mushrooms**, 1 sliced **small onion** and 150 g (5¹/₂ oz/1 cup) grated **mozzarella**. You can add a sprinkling of **dried herbs** if you like. Place on the heated baking tray and cook for 10–15 minutes, or until the bottom of the pizza is dark golden and the cheese bubbly hot. Serves 2.

lasagne sheets

three ways with

tomato and spinach lasagne

Have your oven hot and ready at 180°C (350°F/Gas 4). Heat 40 g (1¹/₂ oz) **butter** in a saucepan. When it sizzles, add 2 tablespoons **plain (all-purpose) flour** and stir off the heat for a minute, until it's a thick paste. Return to the heat and gradually pour in 500 ml (17 fl oz/2 cups) **milk**, whisking all the while over a medium heat, until you have a smooth sauce, a bit like a thick custard. Stir through 150 g (5¹/₂ oz/1 cup) grated **mozzarella** and set aside. Line the bottom of a 2–2.5 litre (70–87 fl oz/ 8–10 cup) baking dish with **fresh lasagne sheets**. Top with 125 g (4¹/₂ oz) defrosted frozen **English spinach**, 2 thinly sliced **tomatoes** and a third of the sauce. Repeat once more, finishing with a layer of lasagne and the remaining sauce. Sprinkle over 50 g (1³/₄ oz/ ¹/₂ cup) grated **parmesan** and bake for 40 minutes, until golden.

hand-cut pasta with nutty sage butter

Roll up each of the **fresh lasagne sheets** from a 375 g (13 oz) packet into logs and slice each into 2 cm (³/₄ inch) wide strips. Cook in boiling water for a few minutes, until they rise to the top. Drain and return to the warm pan. Heat 60 g (2¹/₄ oz) **butter** in a frying pan and, when it is sizzling and frothy, add 80 g (2³/₄ oz/¹/₂ cup) **pine nuts** and 4–6 **sage leaves** to the pan. Shake the pan over the heat until the nuts and butter are golden. Add to the pasta with 50 g (1³/₄ oz/¹/₂ cup) grated **parmesan**, then toss together with **sea salt** and **black pepper**.

zucchini and ricotta cannelloni

Have your oven hot and ready at 200°C (400°F/Gas 6). Cook 2 grated **zucchini (courgettes)** and 2 chopped **garlic cloves** in a splash of **olive oil** for 4–5 minutes, so the zucchini sizzles and softens. Remove to a bowl and add 500 g (1 lb 2 oz/2 cups) **ricotta** and 1 handful **flat-leaf (Italian) parsley**, chopped. Season well and stir to evenly combine. Take 2 **fresh lasagne sheets** and cut across the width to give 4 pieces. Divide the ricotta mixture between the sheets of pasta and roll up to form 4 large logs. Place the logs to fit snugly in a buttered ceramic dish. Pour over 250 ml (9 fl oz/1 cup) **tomato-based pasta sauce**, sprinkle with 50 g (1³/₄ oz/¹/₂ cup) grated **parmesan** and bake for 30 minutes.

MASCARPONE
ITALIAN STYLE CREAM CHEESE
MASCARPONE
ITALIAN STYLE CREAM CHEESE
MASCARPONE
ITALIAN STYLE CREAM CHEESE
MASCARPONE
ITALIAN STYLE CREAM CHEESE
MASCARPONE
ITALIAN STYLE CREAM CHEESE

mascarpone is also used in a recipe on page...
151.

mascarpone

three ways with

mascarpone and gorgonzola linguine

Cook 300 g (10^1/$_2$ oz) linguine in boiling water for 8–10 minutes then drain well. Meanwhile, heat 110 g (3^3/$_4$ oz/^{1}/$_2$ cup) mascarpone in a frying pan, stirring over a gentle heat, until warm. Stir through 75 g (2^1/$_2$ oz/^{1}/$_2$ cup) crumbled gorgonzola or blue cheese and a light splash of milk and stir until the cheese is melted smoothly into the warm cream. Add the sauce to the pasta and serve as a starter sprinkled with 1 tablespoon lightly toasted and chopped walnuts.

espresso mousse

Whisk 3 egg whites and 3 tablespoons caster (superfine) sugar in a bowl until firmly peaking. Add 250 ml (9 fl oz/1 cup) pouring (whipping) cream and beat until thick and creamy. Add 110 g (3^3/$_4$ oz/^{1}/$_2$ cup) mascarpone and 4 tablespoons cold espresso coffee and beat until well combined. Spoon the mixture into a bowl and chill. Top with 3 tablespoons toasted flaked almonds.

orange maple mascarpone

Separate 2 eggs and beat the whites to stiff peaks. Beat the yolks with 220 g (7^3/$_4$ oz/1 cup) mascarpone, 2 tablespoons maple syrup and 2 teaspoons finely grated orange zest for a few minutes until smooth and a little thickened. Fold through the egg whites. Serve with a fruit salad, grilled peaches or as a dip for fresh figs.

mayonnaise is also used in recipes on pages...
35, 161, 189 and 213.

mayonnaise

three ways with

anchovy and caper mayonnaise

Put 250 g (9 oz/1 cup) good-quality **mayonnaise** in a food processor with 6–8 **anchovy fillets** and 1 teaspoon of **oil** from the anchovies, 1 crushed **garlic clove** and 1 tablespoon rinsed **capers** and blend for 10 seconds. Put in a bowl and stir through 2 tablespoons finely chopped **flat-leaf (Italian) parsley**. Add some **black pepper** and a squeeze of **lemon juice**. Serve a generous dollop with pan-fried **veal cutlets** or as a salad dressing.

asian coleslaw

Combine 125 g (4½ oz/½ cup) **mayonnaise**, 2 tablespoons **rice vinegar**, 1 teaspoon **mild mustard** and 2 teaspoons **sesame oil** in a bowl and stir until smooth. Combine 180 g (6½ oz/4 cups) finely shredded **Chinese cabbage**, 1 grated **carrot**, 130 g (4¾ oz/ 1 cup) grated **daikon**, 4 finely sliced **spring onions (scallions)**, and 2 handfuls chopped **coriander (cilantro) leaves and stems** in a large bowl. Add the mayonnaise to the salad and toss well to evenly combine.

chicken mayonnaise salad

Shred the meat and skin of a **barbecued chicken** and put in a bowl with 2 sliced **celery stalks**, 1 tablespoon rinsed **capers**, 70 g (2½ oz/½ cup) halved **pitted black olives**, 1 handful chopped **flat-leaf (Italian) parsley**, 2 chopped **hard-boiled eggs** and 250 g (9 oz/1 cup) **mayonnaise**. Toss to evenly combine the ingredients. Serve the salad with lightly toasted **rye bread**.

mayonnaise / fridge

mozzarella is also used in recipes on pages...
37, 39 and 99.

mozzarella

three ways with

mozzarella and prosciutto tortilla

Sprinkle 150 g (5½ oz/1 cup) grated **mozzarella** over a soft **tortilla** or **burrito** and lay 3–4 thin slices of **prosciutto** and a small handful of **basil** on top. Generously grind over some **black pepper** and place another **tortilla** or **burrito** on top. Heat a non-stick frying pan to high and cook the tortilla or burrito for 2–3 minutes each side, until golden and crisp. Cut into wedges and serve. Serves 1.

tomato, pesto and mozzarella pizza

Have your oven hot and ready at 220°C (425°F/Gas 7). Spread 1 tablespoon good-quality **pesto** on a small, round **Greek** or **Egyptian bread** and top with 1 sliced **tomato** and 6 thin slices of **mozzarella**. Grind over some **black pepper** and place on a tray and into the oven for 10 minutes. Top with some **basil** and a drizzle of **olive oil**. Serves 1.

asparagus and mozzarella omelette

Cut the ends off a bunch of **asparagus** and cut each spear into 3 cm (1¼ inch) lengths. Heat a splash of **olive oil** in a non-stick frying pan and stir-fry the asparagus for 2–3 minutes. Have your grill (broiler) hot and ready. Beat 3 **eggs** in a bowl and add 75 g (2½ oz/½ cup) cubed **mozzarella** and the asparagus and season well with **sea salt** and **black pepper**. Heat 1 tablespoon **olive oil** in a small non-stick frying pan, swirling the pan around to coat in the oil, and pour the egg mixture evenly into the pan. Sprinkle with 3 tablespoons grated **parmesan** and cook for 3–4 minutes, so the edges puff, and place under the grill (broiler) and cook until golden on top. Serves 1.

parmesan is also used in recipes on pages...
13, 19, 23, 27, 39, 45, 55, 71, 79, 81, 87, 89, 91, 93, 107, 149, 159, 173, 175, 193 and 197.

parmesan

three ways with

nutty red pesto

Put 1 **red capsicum (pepper)** over an open gas flame for 8–10 minutes, turning often so it evenly blackens (or put it on a baking tray and blast it in a really hot oven until blistered all over). Put in a plastic bag for a few minutes to cool. Peel off the skin, discard the seeds and place the flesh in a food processor with 80 g (2³/4 oz/¹/2 cup) lightly toasted **cashews**, 3 tablespoons lightly toasted **pine nuts**, 1 seeded **small red chilli** (optional), 3 tablespoons **olive oil**, a really good squeeze of **lemon juice** and **sea salt** and **black pepper**. Blend to a paste and remove to a bowl, then stir through a generous serve of grated **parmesan**.

parmesan and garlic spaghetti

Place 4 tablespoons good **fruity olive oil** and 4 chopped **garlic cloves** in a frying pan over a gentle heat. As soon as the garlic starts to sizzle, remove from the heat and allow to rest and soften in the pan, intensely flavouring the oil. Cook 400 g (14 oz) **spaghetti** (or other thin pasta such as linguine) in boiling water for 8–10 minutes. Drain well and return to the warm pan. Add the garlic oil and 50 g (1³/4 oz/¹/2 cup) grated **parmesan** and season well with **sea salt** and **black pepper**. Toss around well to combine the flavours. Enjoy as a tasty starter.

chilli parmesan asparagus

Boil some water in a frying pan and cook 350 g (12 oz) **asparagus**, trimmed, in the boiling water for 2 minutes. Drain well and return the asparagus to the warm pan with 40 g (1¹/2 oz) **butter**, 3 tablespoons **breadcrumbs**, ¹/2 teaspoon **chilli flakes** and a good grinding of **black pepper**. Shake the pan for a few minutes so the butter melts and the crumbs turn an even golden colour. Sprinkle over 3 tablespoons finely grated **parmesan** and place under a hot grill (broiler) for just a minute or two until the parmesan starts to turn golden. Serve as a starter or a side dish.

parmesan / fridge

ricotta is also used in recipes on pages...
39, 71, 81, 87, 91, 167 and 173.

ricotta

three ways with

herb and chilli ricotta

Put 500 g (1 lb 2 oz/2 cups) ricotta in a food processor with 1 teaspoon chilli flakes, 3 tablespoons roughly chopped flat-leaf (Italian) parsley, 2 tablespoons roughly chopped dill, 2 teaspoons grated lemon zest, 2 tablespoons snipped chives and a generous amount of sea salt and black pepper (ricotta really needs a good seasoning). Combine until smooth, but don't over-mix. You still want to see the nice fresh flecks of herbs. Spoon into 4 individual serving cups, cover and chill until needed. Enjoy as a starter with garlic bread or toss through pasta.

ricotta, tomato and basil pasta salad

Put 4 chopped ripe and tasty tomatoes in a large bowl with 3 tablespoons good fruity olive oil, 2 crushed garlic cloves, a large handful of torn basil, 1 teaspoon sea salt and a good pinch of sugar, toss around to combine and set aside for 20 minutes, to allow the flavours to develop. Meanwhile, cook 400 g (14 oz) penne in boiling water for 8–10 minutes. Drain well. Add the pasta to the tomatoes with 250 g (9 oz/1 cup) fresh ricotta, tossing well to really combine all the flavours. Add some freshly ground black pepper and serve.

ricotta and winter green pasta sauce

Heat 1 tablespoon olive oil in a saucepan and cook 2 sliced leeks and 2 grated zucchini (courgettes) for 5–6 minutes, so the vegetables are silky soft. Add 2–3 large handfuls of chopped cavolo nero or silverbeet (swiss chard) and cook for another 2–3 minutes, until the greens are wilted and dark green. Put in a bowl with 500 g (1 lb 2 oz/2 cups) fresh ricotta, season well and toss through your favourite pasta.

ricotta / fridge

soft tofu is also used in a recipe on page...
135.

soft tofu

three ways with

grandma's tofu and pork hotpot

Place a 300 g (10½ oz) block of soft (silken) tofu on some paper towel to drain any excess liquid. Cut into 2 cm (¾ inch) cubes and place on several layers of paper towel. Heat a good splash of vegetable oil in a heavy-based casserole dish and cook 2 chopped garlic cloves and 2 teaspoons grated ginger for a few seconds so they just flavour the oil but don't burn. Add 300 g (10½ oz) minced (ground) pork and stir-fry for 3–4 minutes, so the pork is no longer pink. Quickly combine 500 ml (17 fl oz/2 cups) chicken stock, 2 tablespoons oyster sauce, 2 teaspoons cornflour (cornstarch) and a pinch of sugar and salt in a bowl and pour into the pan. Bring to the boil, so it thickens a little and add 80 g (2¾ oz/½ cup) peas. Place on a lid and cook on a low heat for 2–3 minutes. Add the tofu and gently stir through, being careful not to break up the tofu. Serve with a sprinkling of white pepper.

silky fried tofu with chilli pepper and lemon

Place a 600 g (1 lb 5 oz) block of soft (silken) tofu on some paper towel to drain any excess liquid. Combine 1 teaspoon black pepper, 1 teaspoon chilli flakes and 1 tablespoon sea salt in a bowl. Cut the tofu into 2–3 cm (¾–1¼ inch) cubes. Place the pieces on some more paper towel while you heat the oil to fry in. Fill a wok half full of oil and heat over a high heat until the surface shimmers gently. Put 125 g (4½ oz/1 cup) cornflour (cornstarch) in a bowl. Dip several pieces of tofu at a time in the flour and directly into the hot oil and fry for 1–2 minutes, until nicely golden. Place the cooked tofu on a plate, sprinkle with the seasoning and serve with a scattering of chopped coriander (cilantro) leaves and stems and a generous amount of lemon wedges on the side.

steamed tofu with ginger and spring onion

Place a 600 g (1 lb 5 oz) block of soft (silken) tofu on some paper towel to drain any excess liquid. Cut into 3 cm (1¼ inch) cubes and place in a heatproof bowl. Have a wok of water boiling and a steamer ready to go. Combine 3 tablespoons chicken stock, 1 tablespoon light soy sauce and a good pinch of sugar in a bowl and pour the mixture over the tofu. Place the bowl in the steamer, cover and steam for 10 minutes. Sprinkle 2 teaspoons finely grated ginger and 2 finely sliced spring onions (scallions) over the steamed tofu. Heat 2 tablespoons light cooking oil and 1 teaspoon sesame oil in a saucepan until smoking hot and pour over the tofu so the ginger and spring onions sizzle and flavour the oil.

soft tofu / fridge

sour cream is also used in recipes on pages... 15, 23, 55, 61, 63, 65, 99, 141 and 143.

sour cream

three ways with

winter mash with bacon and sour cream

Stir-fry 2 **bacon slices** and 2 finely chopped **onions** in a splash of sizzling **olive oil** for 4–5 minutes. Add 60 g (2¹/₄ oz) **butter** to the saucepan and stir over a gentle heat to melt the butter. Set aside. Cook 4 peeled and quartered **large potatoes** in a saucepan of boiling water for 20 minutes. Drain and return the potatoes to the hot pan with 125 g (4¹/₂ oz/¹/₂ cup) **sour cream** or **crème fraîche**. Mash for a few minutes then beat with a wooden spoon to really soften and cream the potatoes. Quickly reheat the onion mixture and stir through the potatoes. Taste for seasoning and serve with winter **meat dishes**.

creamy scrambled eggs with dill

Beat 6 **eggs** with 3 tablespoons **sour cream** or **crème fraîche**, a small handful of roughly chopped **dill** and a pinch of **salt**. Heat 40 g (1¹/₂ oz) **butter** in a non-stick frying pan. When the butter is gently sizzling, pour in the egg mixture. Let it cook in the pan without stirring for a minute. When the edges start to puff up, gently fold the eggs towards the centre of the pan. Repeat until the eggs are firm to your liking. Remove from the heat and keep in the warm pan while you toast and butter your **bread**. Serves 2 with **smoked salmon**.

chicken and bacon goulash

Cook 2 chopped **bacon slices** and 1 chopped **onion** in a splash of hot **oil** for 4–5 minutes, so both the bacon and onion sizzle in the hot pan. Add 2 thinly sliced **boneless, skinless chicken breasts** and stir-fry for 5 minutes, to lightly brown the chicken. Add 125 ml (4 fl oz/ ¹/₂ cup) **white wine** to the hot pan so it sizzles. Cook until the wine has almost evaporated and stir through 250 g (9 oz/1 cup) **sour cream** or **crème fraîche**, 2 tablespoons **sun-dried tomato paste (concentrated purée)** and simmer for 5 minutes. Remove from the heat and stir through a handful of chopped **flat-leaf (Italian) parsley**. Serve with **potato mash**, **risoni** or **rice**.

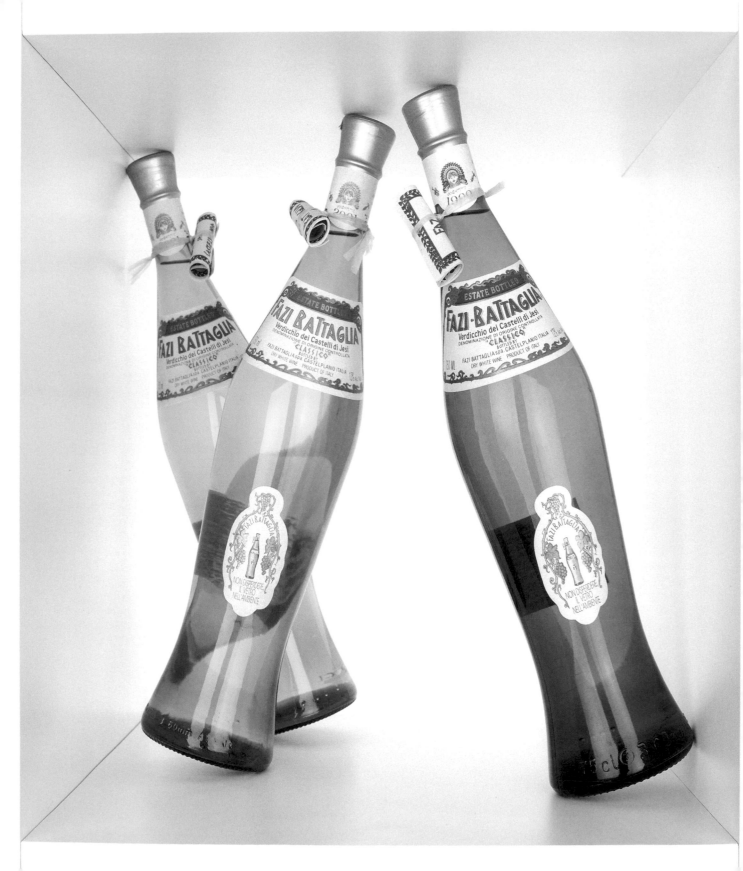

white wine is also used in recipes on pages...
53 and 123.

white wine

three ways with

chicken cacciatore

Heat a few splashes of **light olive oil** in a large heavy-based casserole dish. Cook 4 **chicken forequarters** in the sizzling oil for 5–6 minutes, turning the pieces often, so they are well browned, then remove. Cook 1 chopped **onion**, 2 chopped **garlic cloves**, 1 chopped **carrot** and 1 sliced **celery stalk** in the dish for 2–3 minutes, to soften the vegetables. Add 250 ml (9 fl oz/ 1 cup) **white wine** to the pan and let it sizzle for a few minutes until almost evaporated. Return the chicken to the dish with 400 g (14 oz) tinned **chopped tomatoes**, 90 g (3¼ oz/½ cup) **black olives** and 250 ml (9 fl oz/1 cup) water. Season well, cover and simmer for 50 minutes. Stir through a handful of chopped **flat-leaf (Italian) parsley** and serve with **potato mash** or **soft polenta**.

tipsy lemon risotto

Heat 500 ml (17 fl oz/2 cups) **white wine** and 500 ml (17 fl oz/ 2 cups) **chicken stock** in a saucepan so it simmers gently. Cook 1 chopped **onion** and 2 chopped **garlic cloves** in 40 g (1½ oz) sizzling **butter** until they are softened. Add 330 g (11¾ oz/1½ cups) **risotto rice** and stir-fry for a minute to evenly coat the rice and so it looks shiny. Add 125 ml (4 fl oz/½ cup) of the hot stock to the pan and stir constantly until it has almost all been absorbed. Repeat this process until all the stock is in with the rice and keep stirring until the rice is soft but still has a little bit of a bite to it. Stir in 40 g (1½ oz) **butter**, 50 g (1¾ oz/½ cup) finely grated **parmesan**, a really good squeeze of **lemon juice** and **salt** and **black pepper**. Serve with little more grated **parmesan** on top.

vanilla peaches

Bring 500 ml (17 fl oz/2 cups) **white wine** to the boil and add 220 g (7¾ oz/1 cup) **sugar** and 1 **vanilla bean**, split down the middle so all those tasty, tiny seeds flavour the sweet syrup. Add 4 **small peaches** or 8 **apricots** and simmer for 10 minutes so they are really soft. Put the fruit on a plate and boil the poaching liquid until it has reduced by half then pour over the fruit. Allow the fruit to cool in the syrup. Mix together 125 g (4½ oz/½ cup) **light sour cream** or **crème fraiche** and 1 tablespoon **soft brown sugar** and serve with the peaches.

white wine / fridge

yoghurt is also used in recipes on pages...
67, 87, 123, 139, 147 and 201.

yoghurt

three ways with

turkish cucumber salad

Combine 250 g (9 oz/1 cup) plain yoghurt, 1 teaspoon ground cumin, 1 crushed garlic clove, 1 tablespoon white vinegar and 1 teaspoon sea salt in a bowl. Chop 4 Lebanese (short) cucumbers into 2 cm (3/4 inch) pieces and combine in a large bowl with 2 large handfuls mint. Spoon the yoghurt dressing over the top and serve straight up.

cauliflower in spiced yoghurt

Cook 500 g (1 lb 2 oz/4 cups) cauliflower florets in boiling water for 5 minutes and drain well. Stir-fry 1 chopped onion, 1 chopped garlic clove, 2 teaspoons chopped ginger, 1/2 teaspoon ground ginger and 2 sliced green chillies in a splash of vegetable oil for 5 minutes on a gentle heat. Add the cauliflower pieces and cook for 10 minutes, so the cauliflower slowly begins to turn golden and softens. Add 250 g (9 oz/1 cup) Greek-style yoghurt to the pan and cook over a gentle heat to warm through. Stir through 1/2 teaspoon garam masala and serve with basmati rice and warm naan bread.

smoky eggplant, cumin and mint dip

Prick 1 large eggplant (aubergine) all over with a fork and place it and a whole head of garlic on a baking tray and into a really hot oven for 10–15 minutes, until the eggplant looks puffed up and the garlic quite golden. Remove and allow to cool. Peel the eggplant and put the flesh into a food processor. Cut the garlic in half and squeeze out the soft insides into the food processor with 3 tablespoons tahini, 125 g (41/2 oz/1/2 cup) plain yoghurt, 1 teaspoon ground cumin, a handful of mint, a good squeeze of a lemon and 3 tablespoons olive oil and blend to a chunky consistency. Season well and serve with some fingers of toasted bread.

3 ways with...

ingredients from
the freezer

berries are also used in recipes on pages...
69, 151 and 163.

berries

three ways with

maple berry compote

Defrost 150 g (5 1/2 oz/2 cups) frozen **mixed berries** (try your favourite berry or a combination of a few) in a bowl. Add 2 teaspoons **cornflour (cornstarch)** and stir around well to evenly combine. Bring 125 ml (4 fl oz/ 1/2 cup) **maple syrup** to the boil in a saucepan. Add the berry mixture and stir a few times, reduce the heat to low and simmer for 3–4 minutes, so the liquid is thick and syrupy. Remove from the heat, put in a bowl and allow to cool. Serve dolloped over **pikelets**, **hotcakes** or **thick buttered toast**.

messy berry pav

Sit 500 g (1 lb 2 oz) frozen **mixed berries** (or your favourite frozen berry) in a sieve over a bowl to completely defrost. Put the drained berry juice in a saucepan with 3 tablespoons **sugar**, bring to the boil and simmer for a couple of minutes, until thickened slightly, and allow to cool. Crumble 6 **small meringues** into a ceramic dish (about 8 cm/3 1/4 inches across). Whip up 300 ml (10 1/2 fl oz) **pouring (whipping) cream** with 1 teaspoon **natural vanilla extract** and 60 g (2 1/4 oz/ 1/2 cup) **icing (confectioners') sugar** until the whisk leaves soft peaks when it is removed. Spoon the cream over the meringues. Spoon the berries over the cream and drizzle the syrup all over.

blueberry sour cream pudding

Have your oven hot and ready at 180°C (350°F/Gas 4). Grease a 1–1.5 litre (35–52 fl oz/4–6 cup) baking dish with **butter**. Blend 125 g (4 1/2 oz) very soft **butter** and 185 g (6 1/2 oz/1 cup) **soft brown sugar** in a food processor for 2 minutes, until smooth. With the motor running, add 1 **egg** and blend for a few seconds. Add 300 g (10 1/2 oz) **light sour cream** or **crème fraîche** and blend until smoothly combined with the other ingredients. With the motor running, slowly add 125 g (4 1/2 oz/1 cup) **self-raising flour** until it is all smoothly combined. Put in a bowl and quickly stir through 150 g (5 1/2 oz/1 cup) frozen **blueberries**. Spoon into the baking dish and put into the oven for 1 hour. It will still be soft in the centre. Serve with **custard** or **vanilla ice cream**.

broad beans are also used in a recipe on page...
21.

broad beans

three ways with

broad bean, artichoke and marinated feta salad

Cook 310 g (11 oz/2 cups) frozen **broad beans** in boiling water for 5 minutes. Drain, remove the skins and put in a bowl with 3 tablespoons **olive oil** and 1 tablespoon **red wine vinegar**. Add 6 halved **marinated** or **grilled artichokes** and 2–3 handfuls **baby rocket (arugula) leaves**. Toss all around to combine and evenly coat in the dressing. Top with 150 g (5½ oz/1 cup) crumbled **marinated feta** and sprinkle over 2 tablespoons roughly chopped **dill**. This makes a great side to **grilled lamb**.

creamy broad bean mash

Defrost and peel 310 g (11 oz/ 2 cups) frozen **broad beans**. Cook 1 peeled and roughly chopped **potato** in boiling water for 10 minutes. Add the beans and cook for a further 5 minutes. Drain and return to the warm pan with 40 g (1½ oz) **butter** and 2 tablespoons **milk** and mash until combined but still chunky. Season really well and serve with **grilled lamb**, **tuna steaks** or as part of an antipasto platter.

broad bean and avocado guacamole

Peel 310 g (11 oz/2 cups) frozen **broad beans** and cook in boiling water for 10 minutes. Drain and peel, then put in a food processor with a couple of tablespoons of boiling water and process to a smooth paste. Put in a bowl and add 1 **avocado**, 250 g (9 oz/1 cup) **light sour cream** or **crème fraîche**, 1 chopped **small red onion**, 1 small handful chopped **coriander (cilantro) leaves**, a squeeze of **lime juice** and a dash of **Tabasco**. Mash until combined but still chunky. Season well and enjoy as a dip with warm **bread** or a side to **nachos** or Mexican-flavoured dishes.

corn is also used in a recipe on page... 109.

corn

three ways with

golden cornbread

Have your oven hot and ready at 200°C (400°F/Gas 6). Combine 125 g (4¹/₂ oz/1 cup) plain (all-purpose) flour, 150 g (5¹/₂ oz/ 1 cup) polenta, 1 tablespoon baking powder with a generous pinch of salt and sugar in a bowl. Make a well in the centre. Combine 250 ml (9 fl oz/1 cup) milk, 250 g (9 oz/1 cup) light sour cream or crème fraîche, 3 eggs and 300 g (10¹/₂ oz/2 cups) frozen corn in a bowl and add to the flour mixture. Stir for a minute, but don't overmix. Heat a generous splash of light olive oil in an ovenproof frying pan or casserole dish and swirl around to coat the bottom of the pan. When smoking hot, pour in the corn batter and cook for 1 minute, letting it sizzle in the pan. Cook in the oven for 25 minutes, or until golden and puffed. Remove and allow to cool for a few minutes before turning out onto a larger plate or chopping board. Cut into wedges or squares to serve.

corn fritters

Put 150 g (5¹/₂ oz/1 cup) defrosted frozen corn in a bowl with 3 chopped spring onions (scallions), 125 g (4¹/₂ oz/¹/₂ cup) sour cream or crème fraîche, 2 eggs, 60 g (2¹/₄ oz/¹/₂ cup) self-raising flour and a good seasoning of salt and black pepper. Stir until evenly combined and the batter is smooth and thickly coats the corn. Heat a splash of vegetable oil in a frying pan. Spoon in 2 tablespoons of the mixture to make a fritter and cook for 2–3 minutes each side, until golden. This mixture makes 8 fritters to enjoy with bacon, eggs and home-style tomato relish.

corn, capsicum and coriander stir-fry

Heat a good splash of vegetable oil in a hot wok and stir-fry 2 chopped garlic cloves and 3 chopped spring onions (scallions) for a few seconds to flavour the oil. Add 1 sliced red capsicum (pepper), stir-fry for 1 minute then add 300 g (10¹/₂ oz/ 2 cups) defrosted frozen corn. Stir-fry for 3–4 minutes then add 2 large handfuls chopped coriander (cilantro) leaves, 2 tablespoons light soy sauce and 1 tablespoon red wine vinegar. Stir, cover with a lid and cook for 2 minutes. Serves 2.

filo

three ways with

mushroom and feta pie

Have your oven hot and ready at 180°C (350°F/Gas 4). Melt 60 g (2 1/4 oz) **butter** and set aside. Lay 4 sheets of **filo** on top of each other, brushing the melted butter between each sheet. Place the sheets in a 22–25 cm (8 1/2–10 inch) round baking dish or cake tin, letting the long ends overlap. Repeat the process with 4 more sheets of **filo** but lay them in the dish in the opposite direction. Remove the stems from 4 **large flat mushrooms** and cut the caps in quarters. Place the mushroom pieces over the filo and scatter 150 g (5 1/2 oz/1 cup) roughly crumbled **feta** on top. Beat 3 **eggs** in a bowl with 125 ml (4 fl oz/ 1/2 cup) **pouring (whipping) cream** and a good grinding of **black pepper**. Pour over the mushrooms. Fold over the edges of the filo and gently crush to make a rustic border. Brush with any remaining butter and bake for 30 minutes, until the pastry is crisp and golden.

lamb and feta filo parcels

Have your oven hot and ready at 180°C (350°F/Gas 4). Season 4 **lamb leg roasting fillets** (about 185 g/6 1/2 oz each) really well. Heat a splash of **olive oil** in a very hot frying pan and cook the lamb for 4 minutes, turning every minute, until brown all over. Remove and allow to cool. Mash 4 tablespoons **soft feta** (try a marinated feta) with a fork and rub over the lamb. Place 1 sheet of **filo** on top of another and place 1 piece of lamb running along the short end. Brush the edges with a little melted butter. Fold along the length, folding in the sides as you go, to make a neat parcel. Repeat to make 4. Place on a tray and bake for 25 minutes, until golden. Serve with a simple **tomato, red onion and mint salad**.

salmon dill pie

Have your oven hot and ready at 180°C (350°F/Gas 4). Melt 60 g (2 1/4 oz) **butter**. Lay 4 sheets of **filo** on a flat surface, brushing between each layer with the butter. Put 400 g (14 oz) tinned, drained **red salmon** in a bowl and roughly mash. Add 250 g (9 oz/ 1 cup) **Greek-style yoghurt**, 1 tablespoon finely chopped **dill**, 2 **eggs**, 75 g (2 3/4 oz/1/2 cup) crumbled **feta** and a good squeeze of **lemon juice**, and season well. Spoon the mixture to fit into a small ovenproof dish. Carefully place the filo on top, fold over the edges and gently crush up, to give a rustic effect, and bake for 25–30 minutes, until golden.

ice cream is also used in a recipe on page... 157.

ice cream

three ways with

tutti-frutti ice cream

Soften 1 litre (35 fl oz/4 cups) vanilla ice cream. Blend 315 g (11 oz/1 cup) roughly chopped mango flesh with 2 tablespoons icing (confectioners') sugar in a food processor until smooth. Add to the ice cream along with 3 tablespoons passionfruit pulp, stirring quickly to combine. Spoon into a freezer container and into the freezer until firm.

adults only affogato

Place 2 scoops of vanilla ice cream each into 4 glasses and keep in the freezer until needed. To serve, make 250 ml (9 fl oz/ 1 cup) hot strong coffee. Pour 1 tablespoon of liqueur over each serve of the ice cream (try grappa, Frangelico or Grand Marnier), top with a quarter of the coffee for each serve and enjoy.

strawberry meringue parfait

Soften 1 litre (35 fl oz/4 cups) vanilla ice cream in a large bowl. Put 250 g (9 oz/1²/₃ cups) hulled strawberries and 1 tablespoon icing (confectioners') sugar in a food processor and blend until the strawberries are finely chopped, then add to the ice cream. Roughly break up meringues to give about 2 cups in volume and put in the ice cream bowl. Stir to evenly combine the ingredients. Spoon into a loaf (bar) tin and freeze. When firm, remove from the tin and cut into thick slices.

peas are also used in recipes on pages...
15, 51, 115, 119, 137 and 147.

peas

pea curry

Cook 1 chopped **onion**,
1 teaspoon grated **ginger** and
1 chopped **large red chilli** in a
splash of **vegetable oil** until the
onion softens and gently sizzles
in the oil. Add 2 tablespoons **mild
curry powder** and cook for a
minute, to release the hidden
spices in the powder. Add
3 chopped **tomatoes** and 250 ml
(9 fl oz/1 cup) water and bring to
the boil. Add 155 g (5¹/₂ oz/1 cup)
frozen **peas**, return to the boil and
reduce the heat to a rapid simmer
for 15 minutes, so the sauce has
thickened. Stir through 20 g
(³/₄ oz) **butter**, taste for seasoning
and serve with **rice**.

rigatoni with pea, eggplant and mint sauce

Cook 400 g (14 oz) **rigatoni** in
boiling water for 8–10 minutes.
Drain and return to the warm pan.
Meanwhile, heat 3 tablespoons
olive oil in a frying pan over a high
heat and, when smoking hot, add
1 finely cubed **eggplant (aubergine)**
and cook for 3–4 minutes, until
golden. Add 1 chopped **garlic
clove**, 1 teaspoon **dried mint** and
cook for 1 minute. Add 500 ml
(17 fl oz/2 cups) **tomato passata
(puréed tomatoes)** and 155 g
(5¹/₂ oz/1 cup) defrosted frozen
peas and cook for 4–5 minutes.
Serve over or tossed through the
pasta with **parmesan** or a dollop
of **fresh ricotta**.

pea soup with crispy prosciutto and ricotta toasts

Cook 1 chopped **onion** in 40 g
(1¹/₂ oz) of sizzling **butter** for
2–3 minutes. Add 465 g (1 lb/
3 cups) frozen **peas** and 1 litre
(35 fl oz/4 cups) **chicken stock**
and boil for 10 minutes. Pour into
a food processor and blend for
1 minute, until smooth, and return
to the clean saucepan. Taste for
seasoning and leave on a low heat.
Heat a splash of **olive oil** in a
frying pan and cook 4–6 slices
of **prosciutto** in the hot oil for
2 minutes each side, so they
brown and crisp. Remove from the
pan. Toast 4 slices of **sourdough**
until golden, and thickly spread
3 tablespoons **ricotta** on each slice.
Crumble the prosciutto over the
soup and serve with the toasts.

pizza bases are also used in recipes on pages...
21 and 37.

pizza bases

three ways with

bruschetta pizza with tomato, anchovy and basil

Have your oven hot and ready at 220°C (425°F/Gas 7) and place a baking tray in the oven. Mix together 2 crushed **garlic cloves** and 3 tablespoons **olive oil** and brush over 2 frozen **pizza bases**. Cook the pizzas in the oven for 12–15 minutes, until golden, then set aside. Meanwhile, put 3 roughly chopped ripe and tasty **large tomatoes**, 6–8 chopped **anchovy fillets**, 2 crushed **garlic cloves** and 2–3 tablespoons **olive oil** in a non-stick frying pan. Stir over a low heat for 2–3 minutes, until just warm, to bring out the flavours of the ingredients. Put in a bowl and toss through 1 large handful roughly torn **basil**, season well with **salt** and **black pepper** and arrange over the warm pizza bases.

spicy spanish pizza

Have your oven hot and ready at 220°C (425°F/Gas 7) and place a baking tray in the oven. Spread 1 tablespoon **tomato paste (concentrated purée)** over a **pizza base**. Top with 8 thin slices of **spicy Spanish salami**, 2 roughly chopped **marinated eggplant (aubergine)** slices and 4 sliced **marinated artichokes** (both available from a delicatessen) and 100 g (3½ oz) finely sliced **manchego cheese**. Place on the hot tray and into the oven for 15 minutes.

potato, onion and rosemary pizza

Have your oven hot and ready at 220°C (425°F/Gas 7) and place a baking tray in the oven. Brush a large **pizza base** (about 25 cm/ 10 inches across) with **olive oil** and 1 crushed **galic clove**. Cover the entire base with 1 very thinly sliced **all-purpose potato** (desiree is best). Top with 1 thinly sliced **onion**, 1 teaspoon **rosemary needles** and 1 teaspoon **sea salt** and **black pepper**. Drizzle a little more **oil** over and cook for 20–25 minutes, until the edges of the pizza and the onion are golden and crispy.

prawns are also used in recipes on pages...
25, 31, 115, 117, 121, 135, 147, 197, 199 and 215.

prawns

three ways with

cheat's tom yum soup

Boil 500 ml (17 fl oz/2 cups) water and add 2–3 tablespoons **tom yum paste**. Stir around for 1 minute then add 1 chopped firm **tomato**, 8–10 peeled and deveined **raw prawns (shrimp)**, 4–6 torn **makrut (kaffir lime) leaves**, a large handful of your favourite **mushrooms**, sliced, a handful of halved **baby corn** and 1 tablespoon each **lime juice** and **fish sauce**. Simmer for 5 minutes, until the prawns are pink and curled and serve hot, topped with a handful of **bean sprouts** and extra **fish sauce** on the side.

spicy thai prawns with beans and basil

Top, tail and halve 3 handfuls **green beans** and defrost 500 g (1 lb 2 oz) frozen peeled and deveined **raw prawns (shrimp)**. Heat 125 ml (4 fl oz/¹/2 cup) **vegetable oil** in a frying pan and, when the surface shimmers, add the beans and sizzle in the hot oil for 5 minutes, so they really soften and start to brown. Place on a plate and drain all but a little oil from the pan. Add 2 tablespoons **red curry paste** and stir-fry for 2–3 minutes, until really fragrant. Add the prawns to the pan and cook for 2 minutes each side, so they become pink and curled. Return the beans to the pan with 125 ml (4 fl oz/¹/2 cup) **chicken stock**, 1 tablespoon **fish sauce** and a good pinch of **sugar**. Cook until almost all the liquid has gone and stir through 1 large handful sweet, liquoricey **Thai basil** to serve.

chilli prawn linguine

Defrost 16–20 peeled and deveined **raw large prawns (shrimp)**. Cook 400 g (14 oz) **linguine** in boiling water for 8–10 minutes. Drain and return to the warm pan. Meanwhile, heat 3 tablespoons **olive oil** in a large frying pan and cook the prawns for 2 minutes each side so they sizzle, become pink and curl in the oil. Add 3 **garlic cloves** and 2 seeded and chopped **small red chillies** to the pan, stirring around so they soften and flavour the oil. Add a generous squeeze of **lemon juice**, 1 large handful roughly chopped **flat-leaf (Italian) parsley** and a generous seasoning of **salt** and **black pepper**. Add the pasta and cook over a gentle heat for 2–3 minutes.

Pampas®
puff pastry

Pampas®
puff pastry

MAKE ME
IN **40**
MINUTES

fresh twist on chicken and vegetables for your family

...st on chicken and veget... ...es for your...

puff pastry is also used in recipes on pages...
13, 15, 27, 89, 105, 161 and 213.

puff pastry

three ways with

lamb wellington

Have your oven hot and ready at 220°C (425°F/Gas 7). Toss 4 **lamb leg roasting fillets** (about 185 g/ 6¹/₂ oz each) in a bowl with a splash of **olive oil**, 1 teaspoon **dried oregano** and season with **black pepper**. Cook the pieces in a really hot frying pan for 4 minutes, turning every minute. Remove and allow to cool. Rub 1 tablespoon **olive tapenade** over each piece of lamb and wrap each piece snugly and neatly in a defrosted 12 x 24 cm (4¹/₂ x 9¹/₂ inch) piece of **puff pastry** (half a standard sheet). Brush with **egg yolk** and cut several slits in the top for steam to escape. Place on a lightly oiled baking tray and bake for 25 minutes, until puffed and golden.

puff pastry with tomato, haloumi and mint salad

Have your oven hot and ready at 220°C (425°F/Gas 7). Fold over the edges of a sheet of **puff pastry** to make a 5 mm (¹/₄ inch) border, pressing down with a fork. Bake in the oven for 15 minutes, until puffed and golden. Cover the top of the pastry with 2 thinly sliced **tomatoes** brushed with a little **olive oil**, season well and return to the oven for 5 minutes. Place the tart on a serving plate and top with a handful of **baby rocket (arugula) leaves**, a handful of **mint** and a drizzle of **olive oil**. Heat a splash of **olive oil** in a hot non-stick frying pan and cook 6 thick slices of **haloumi** for 1 minute each side, until golden. Place the grilled haloumi slices over the tart, season with **black pepper** and serve with wedges of **lemon** to squeeze over.

hot apple danish

Have your oven hot and ready at 220°C (425°F/Gas 7). Cut a piece of **puff pastry** into 4 squares and fold over the edges to make a 5 mm (¹/₄ inch) border. Place on a baking tray lined with baking paper. Peel and core 2 **apples** and cut each into 8 wedges. Cook the wedges in a frying pan with 20 g (³/₄ oz) sizzling **butter**, 2 tablespoons **caster (superfine) sugar** and ¹/₂ teaspoon **natural vanilla extract** for 4–5 minutes, turning often so the apples start to soften. Place the apple wedges on the pastry and cook for 20 minutes, so the pastry is puffed and golden. Serve hot with **custard** and **vanilla ice cream**.

Pampas® **5** ready rolled sheets shortcrust pastry

Pampas® **5** ready rolled sheets shortcrust pastry

shortcrust pastry

three ways with

savoury lamb pie

Have your oven hot and ready at 180°C (350°F/Gas 4). Cook 1 chopped **onion** in a splash of **light olive oil** for a few minutes, sizzling gently in the oil to soften. Add 500 g (1 lb 2 oz) **minced (ground) lamb** and stir-fry over a high heat for 5 minutes so the lamb browns. Add 155 g (5½ oz/ 1 cup) **peas**, 2 **carrots**, 1 teaspoon **dried oregano**, 500 ml (17 fl oz/ 2 cups) **beef stock** mixed with 1 tablespoon **cornflour (cornstarch)** and 2 tablespoons **worcestershire sauce**. Bring the mixture to the boil for a few minutes, until the sauce thickens. Pour into a baking dish. Top with a sheet of **shortcrust pastry**, trim to fit and press firmly around the edges. Brush with an **egg yolk** mixed with a splash of cold water and bake for 30 minutes, until the pastry is golden.

provençal tomato and cheese tart

Have your oven hot and ready at 180°C (350°F/Gas 4). Defrost a sheet of **shortcrust pastry** and place on a lightly oiled baking sheet. Press around the edges with a fork to mark a border and bake for 10 minutes and allow to cool. Lay thin slices of **gruyère** or **edam** over the entire tart, top with 2 thinly sliced ripe **tomatoes**, ½ teaspoon **dried basil**, 2 tablespoons grated **parmesan** and a good seasoning of **salt** and **black pepper**. Dot 40 g (1½ oz) **butter** on top and bake for 20–25 minutes.

asparagus and goat's cheese tart

Have your oven hot and ready at 180°C (350°F/Gas 4). Cut a sheet of frozen **shortcrust pastry** in half and place on a lightly oiled baking tray. Fold over the edges just a little to make a thin border and bake for 15 minutes. Remove and cool. Cut 2 bunches of **thin asparagus** into 10 cm (4 inch) long stalks. Put in a frying pan with 40 g (1½ oz) **butter**, season well and toss around over a high heat in the sizzling butter for 3–4 minutes. Crumble 3 tablespoons **goat's cheese** over the base of each tart, top with the asparagus and 4 tablespoons grated **parmesan**. Bake for 20 minutes. Serves 2.

shortcrust pastry / freezer

spinach is also used in a recipe on page...
39.

spinach

three ways with

shell pasta with ricotta and spinach

Have your oven hot and ready at 180°C (350°F/Gas 4). Cook 400 g (14 oz) small shell pasta in boiling water for 8–10 minutes, drain and return to the warm pot. Meanwhile, put 200 g (7 oz) defrosted frozen spinach in a large bowl with 750 g (1 lb 10 oz/3 cups) ricotta, 100 g (3½ oz/1 cup) grated parmesan and a generous seasoning of salt and black pepper. Stir to combine and add to the pot with the pasta, stirring well to combine. Spoon into a 3 litre (104 fl oz/12 cup) greased baking dish, top with some extra grated parmesan and bake for 30 minutes.

spinach and chickpea curry

Cook 1 chopped red onion and 2 chopped garlic cloves in a splash of vegetable oil for 5 minutes, so the onion gently sizzles and softens. Add 1–2 tablespoons of your favourite curry powder or mild Indian curry paste and cook for 2 minutes, stir-frying the paste to bring out the spices. Add 400 g (14 oz) tinned chickpeas, drained and rinsed, 400 g (14 oz) tinned chopped tomatoes, 4–6 finely chopped sun-dried tomatoes and 250 ml (9 fl oz/1 cup) water and boil for 10 minutes. Add 200 g (7 oz) defrosted frozen spinach and gently simmer for 5 minutes. Serve with basmati rice and yoghurt on the side.

creamy spinach and leek soup

Cook 2 sliced leeks in 40 g (1½ oz) gently sizzling butter for 5 minutes so the leeks become soft and silky. Add 2 peeled and chopped large potatoes and 750 ml (26 fl oz/3 cups) chicken stock and boil for 10 minutes. Add 200 g (7 oz) defrosted frozen spinach and cook for a further 5 minutes. Put the mixture in a food processor and blend until smooth. Return to the saucepan, stir through 250 ml (9 fl oz/1 cup) pouring (whipping) cream and cook on a gentle heat for 5 minutes.

vine leaves
three ways with

barbecued haloumi in vine leaves

Wrap a 1 cm ($^1/_2$ inch) thick slice of **haloumi** firmly in **vine leaves**, leaving a little bit of haloumi sticking out either side of the parcel. Cook each parcel on a really hot barbecue hotplate or in a non-stick frying pan with a splash of **fruity olive oil** until the vine leaves go dark green and crispy and sizzle in the oil. Arrange on a platter with a good squeeze of **lemon juice** and enjoy as a starter.

steamed vine leaf fish with dill and lemon

Place several overlapping **vine leaves** on a chopping board to make a 20 cm (8 inch) square. Place a **white fish fillet** (about 180–200 g/ $6^1/_2$–7 oz), skin side down, in the centre of the leaves. Spread 20 g ($^3/_4$ oz) **butter** over the top of the fish, place 2 thin slices of **lemon** on the butter with a sprig of **dill** on the lemon. Season well with **sea salt** and **black pepper** and firmly fold up the edges of the vine leaves to tightly seal. Repeat to make 4 parcels. Place the parcels in a large bamboo steamer and cover with the lid. Place the steamer over a wok or large saucepan of boiling water and steam for 15 minutes.

baked mushrooms and goat's cheese in vine leaves

Drizzle some **fruity olive oil** over the bottom of a small baking tray. Lay 4 **vine leaves** on the base of the tray, so they overlap a little. Remove the stems from 4 **large field mushrooms** and sit them on the vine leaves with 1 tablespoon **soft goat's cheese** in the cap of each mushroom. Drizzle with **olive oil** and a good squeeze of **lemon juice** and top with some freshly ground **black pepper**. Place 4 **vine leaves** on top and bake in a hot oven for 20 minutes. Serve as a starter.

3 ways with...

ingredients from the pantry

almonds are also used in recipes on pages...
35, 41, 117, 123 and 151.

almonds

three ways with

stir-fried chicken with almonds

Cut 6 **chicken thigh fillets** into quarters and toss around in a bowl with 1 tablespoon **cornflour (cornstarch)**, 2 tablespoons **rice wine** (or white wine) and 2 teaspoons **soy sauce**. Set aside for 10 minutes. Heat 3 tablespoons **vegetable oil** in a wok and, when smoking hot, add half of the chicken and stir-fry for 3–4 minutes then remove to a plate. Repeat with the remaining chicken. Remove all but 1 tablespoon of the oil from the wok and stir-fry 2 chopped **garlic cloves**, 45 g (1³/4 oz/¹/2 cup) **flaked** or **slivered almonds** and 2 sliced **celery stalks** for 1 minute. Add a splash of **rice wine** so it sizzles. Return the chicken to the wok, stir-fry for a few minutes and serve with some finely sliced **spring onion (scallion)** on top.

almond and parsley pesto

Put 155 g (5¹/2 oz/1 cup) lightly toasted **almonds** in a food processor with 2 large handfuls **flat-leaf (Italian) parsley**, 2 large handfuls **basil** and 2 tablespoons **lemon juice**. Combine until roughly chopped and, with the motor running, add 4 tablespoons **olive oil**. Season with **salt** and **black pepper** and stir through 50 g (1³/4 oz/¹/2 cup) finely grated **parmesan**. Toss through any **pasta**, little **boiled potatoes** or serve as a side to **chargrilled salmon steaks**. You can also add 250 g (9 oz/1 cup) **ricotta** and use for a pasta sauce.

buttery chicken and almond curry

Chop 4 **chicken thigh fillets** into large bite-sized pieces and cook the pieces in a few splashes of sizzling **vegetable oil** for 5–6 minutes. Add 1 chopped **onion** and stir-fry for a few minutes to soften. Add 3 tablespoons **chicken tikka curry paste** and stir-fry for 3–4 minutes, to release all the aromatic spices in the paste. Add 250 g (9 oz/1 cup) **plain yoghurt** to the pan, 1 tablespoon at a time, stirring well between each addition. When all the yoghurt is incorporated, stir through 125 ml (4 fl oz/¹/2 cup) **pouring (whipping) cream**, 60 g (2¹/4 oz) **butter** and 55 g (2 oz/¹/2 cup) **ground almonds** (saving some to sprinkle on top). Cook over a low heat for a few minutes and serve this rich curry with **basmati rice**.

anchovies are also used in recipes on pages...
35, 43, 73, 103, 105, 149, 183, 191, 197 and 205.

anchovies

three ways with

olive, tomato and anchovy tart

Have your oven hot and ready at 220°C (425°F/Gas 7). Fold over the edges of a sheet of **puff pastry** to make a 1 cm (½ inch) border and place on a tray and into the oven for 10 minutes. Remove and spoon over 3 tablespoons **olive tapenade**, smoothing down, and top with 2 finely sliced **tomatoes** and 4–6 **anchovy fillets** (or to taste, depending how much you like them). Return to the oven for 5–8 minutes so the edges of the pastry are puffed. Remove, scatter with torn **basil** and drizzle with some good **olive oil**. Serves 2.

jansson's temptation

Have your oven hot and ready at 180°C (350°F/Gas 4). Peel and finely slice 3 **large all-purpose potatoes** and 1 **onion**. Place several layers of potatoes and onion slices in a small baking dish with 3–4 **anchovy fillets** between each layer. Heat 125 ml (4 fl oz/ ½ cup) **thick (double/heavy) cream**, 125 ml (4 fl oz/½ cup) **milk**, 20 g (¾ oz) **butter** and a good pinch of **white pepper** in a saucepan until it just about boils and pour over the potatoes. Cook in the oven for 1 hour, so the top layer of potatoes are golden and crispy and the underneath potatoes are soft and creamy. Serve this classic Scandinavian dish with **roast pork** or **lamb**.

chilli tomato risoni

Cook 1 chopped **onion**, 1 chopped **garlic clove** and 4 **anchovy fillets** in a splash of **olive oil** so the onion gently sizzles and softens. Add 200 g (7 oz/1 cup) **risoni** and 1 teaspoon **chilli flakes** and stir around for a minute to really coat the risoni in the tasty oil. Add 400 g (14 oz) tinned **chopped tomatoes**, 500 ml (17 fl oz/2 cups) **chicken stock** and bring to the boil. Place on a lid and cook on a really low heat for 20 minutes. Remove from the heat and leave for a further 5 minutes with the lid on. Stir through a handful of chopped **flat-leaf (Italian) parsley**, a good grinding of **black pepper** and 50 g (1¾ oz/½ cup) grated **parmesan**. Serve with extra grated **parmesan** on top.

artichokes are also used in recipes on pages...
31, 63, 73 and 99.

artichokes

three ways with

artichoke pesto

Put 4 tinned **artichokes** in a food processor with 3 tablespoons lightly toasted **pine nuts**, 1 handful **flat-leaf (Italian) parsley**, roughly chopped, 1 **garlic clove**, 3 tablespoons **light olive oil**, a good squeeze of **lemon juice** and process to a smooth paste. Put in a bowl and stir through 3 tablespoons grated **parmesan**. Add a good seasoning of **sea salt** and **black pepper**. Serve as a condiment to **cheese and crackers**, toss through **pasta** or little **boiled potatoes** or use as a sauce for **grilled fish** or **roast chicken**.

creamy artichoke soup

Place 6 tinned **artichokes**, 1 peeled and finely chopped **large potato** and 750 ml (26 fl oz/3 cups) **chicken stock** in a saucepan and boil for 10 minutes. Put the mixture in a blender and process for about 30 seconds, until smooth. Return the soup to the saucepan, stir through 250 ml (9 fl oz/1 cup) **thick (double/heavy) cream**, season well and gently heat for 2–3 minutes. Spread a little **ricotta** or **blue cheese** on **toast** and serve with the artichoke soup.

fusilli with feta, artichoke and cherry tomato sauce

Cook 400 g (14 oz) **fusilli** in boiling water for 8–10 minutes. Meanwhile, heat a splash of **olive oil** in a frying pan over a high heat and add 2 **garlic cloves** and 250 g (9 oz) **cherry tomatoes**. Cook for 3–4 minutes, shaking the pan, until the tomatoes begin to split. Add 350 g (12 oz) sliced **marinated artichokes**, drained of excess oil, and 2 tablespoons of the tasty **oil** from the artichokes to the pan and cook for a further 2 minutes. Stir through 150 g (5¹/₂ oz/1 cup) crumbled **marinated feta**, a handful of chopped **flat-leaf (Italian) parsley** and some **black pepper**. Add to the pasta, stir to combine and serve. You can also stir through a couple of handfuls of **rocket (arugula)** or **baby English spinach** leaves.

balsamic vinegar is also used in recipes on pages...
35, 97, 189 and 201.

balsamic vinegar

three ways with

balsamic glazed t-bone

Toss 4 **T-bone steaks** in a bowl with 125 ml (4 fl oz/½ cup) **balsamic vinegar**, 2 crushed **garlic cloves** and 2 tablespoons **light soy sauce**. Leave to sit in the marinade for 30 minutes, or cover and refrigerate for a few hours if you have the time. Heat a grill plate or barbecue so it is really hot and cook the steak for 5–6 minutes each side or to your liking. Serve with a simple salad of tossed sliced **tomatoes**, sliced **red onion** and **basil**.

spicy sour tofu

Cut a 600 g (1 lb 5 oz) block of **firm tofu** into 2 cm (¾ in) cubes and place on several layers of paper towel to absorb excess liquid. Heat 250 ml (9 fl oz/1 cup) **vegetable oil** in the wok. When the surface shimmers, add half the tofu and fry for 4–5 minutes, until dark golden. Remove and repeat to cook the remaining tofu. Drain all but 1 tablespoon of oil from the wok and stir-fry 2 seeded and finely chopped **small red chillies**, 2 chopped **garlic cloves** and 3 chopped **spring onions (scallions)** for a few seconds. Add 2 tablespoons **balsamic vinegar**, 2 tablespoons **soy sauce**, 3 tablespoons **chicken stock** and ½ teaspoon **sugar** to the wok and boil for 1 minute. Add the tofu and toss for 1 minute to coat in the spicy dark sauce and serve with **rice** and **Chinese greens**.

spaghetti with balsamic tomatoes

Cook 400 g (14 oz) **spaghetti** in boiling water for 8–10 minutes. Meanwhile, heat a few generous splashes of **olive oil** in a large frying pan over a high heat. Add 4 sliced **garlic cloves** and cook for 1 minute, so the garlic sizzles. Add 500 g (1 lb 2 oz) **cherry tomatoes**, 2 tablespoons **balsamic vinegar** and a sprinkling of **sugar** to the pan, shaking the pan around to cook the tomatoes for 4–5 minutes so they soften and split open. Sprinkle over 1 teaspoon **dried oregano** or 2 sprigs of fresh and stir to combine. Add the pasta to the pan with 2 handfuls **baby rocket (arugula) leaves** and 3 tablespoons grated **parmesan**, tossing around to combine. Serve with extra **parmesan** the side.

balsamic vinegar / pantry

bean thread noodles

chicken noodle hotpot

Chop 3 **skinless, boneless chicken breasts** into bite-sized pieces and toss them in a bowl with 2 teaspoons grated **ginger**, 2 teaspoons **sesame oil** and 2 tablespoons **light soy sauce**. Put 100 g (3¹/₂ oz) **bean thread noodles** in a bowl, cover with boiling water for 8–10 minutes then drain. Put a quarter of a **Chinese cabbage**, chopped into 3 cm (1¹/₄ inch) pieces, in the bottom of a heavy-based casserole dish. Put the noodles on top and the chicken on top of the noodles. Pour over 750 ml (26 fl oz/3 cups) **chicken stock**, slowly bring to the boil then cover and simmer for 15 minutes. Serve topped with 1 large handful chopped **coriander (cilantro) leaves** and 2 sliced **spring onions (scallions)**.

spicy fish soup

Put 100 g (3¹/₂ oz) **bean thread noodles** in a bowl and cover with boiling water for 8–10 minutes, then drain. Put in the bottom of 2 large soup bowls. Boil 1 litre (35 fl oz/4 cups) **fish** or **vegetable stock** and add 2 tablespoons **tom yum paste**, 400 g (14 oz) tinned **chopped tomatoes**, ¹/₂ teaspoon **turmeric** and 1 tablespoon **fish sauce**. Add 300 g (10¹/₂ oz) cubed **white fish fillets** and simmer for 10 minutes. Stir through a handful of chopped **coriander (cilantro) leaves**, 2 tablespoons **lime juice** and pour over the noodles. Serves 2.

spicy pork noodles

Put 100 g (3¹/₂ oz) **bean thread noodles** in a bowl and cover with boiling water for 8–10 minutes, then drain. Heat 2 tablespoons **vegetable oil** in a hot wok and add 3 chopped **spring onions (scallions)**, 1 teaspoon grated **ginger** and 2 teaspoons **Chinese chilli garlic sauce** and stir-fry for just a few seconds. Add 300 g (10¹/₂ oz) **minced (ground) pork** and stir-fry for 5 minutes. Add 250 ml (9 fl oz/1 cup) **chicken stock**, 1 tablespoon **light soy sauce** and a good pinch of **sugar** and **salt**. Stir to combine then add the noodles, tossing all the ingredients around in the wok. Cook for 7–8 minutes, so the sauce thickens and coats the noodles and pork. Serve hot with some extra sliced **spring onions (scallions)** on top.

bean thread noodles / pantry

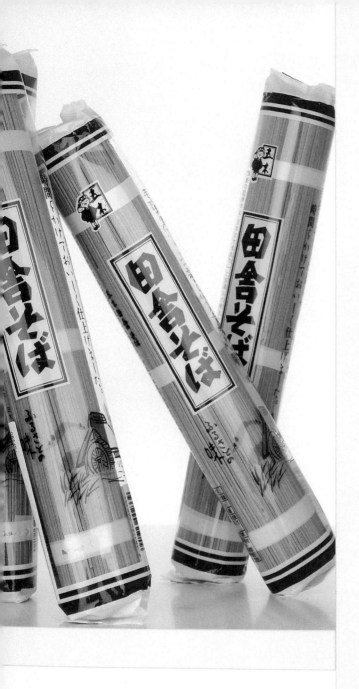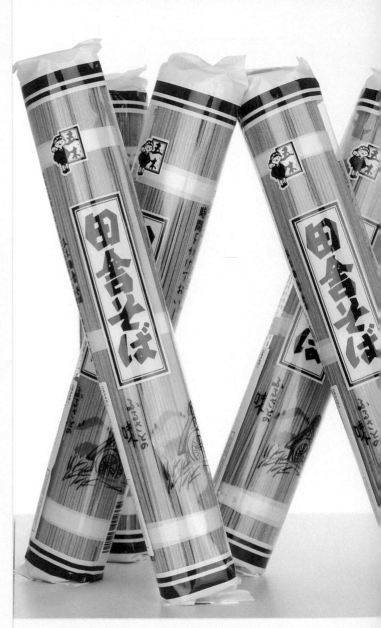

buckwheat noodles

buckwheat noodle salad with grilled lamb, mint and feta

Cook 300 g (10¹/₂ oz) **buckwheat noodles** in boiling water for 3 minutes. Rinse and drain really well, shaking out as much excess water as possible. Toss the noodles with 1 tablespoon of the **oil** from a jar of **soft marinated feta**. Rub **sea salt** and **black pepper** over 2 **lamb backstrap** or **loin fillets** (about 300 g/ 10¹/₂ oz each) and cook the lamb in a splash of hot **vegetable oil** for 3–4 minutes each side, so they are still pink in the middle (or 2 minutes each side if using smaller loin fillets). Remove and rest for 5 minutes before finely slicing across the grain. Add the lamb to the noodles with a handful each of roughly chopped **mint** and **flat-leaf (Italian) parsley**, 150 g (5¹/₂ oz/1 cup) crumbled **marinated feta**, 1 tablespoon of **oil** from the feta and 1 tablespoon **balsamic vinegar**. Gently toss to combine and serve.

japanese mushroom and leek broth

Cook 200 g (7 oz) **buckwheat noodles** in boiling water for 2–3 minutes and drain. Heat a splash of **vegetable oil** and a drizzle of **sesame oil** in a saucepan and stir-fry 1 sliced **leek** for 3–4 minutes. Add 2 handfuls each trimmed **shiitake**, **enoki** and **oyster mushrooms**, and stir-fry to soften for a few minutes. Add 750 ml (26 fl oz/3 cups) **chicken** or **vegetable stock**, 2 tablespoons **light soy sauce** and a ¹/₂ teaspoon **sugar**. Simmer for 5 minutes. Put the noodles in bowls and ladle over the broth.

buckwheat noodles with smoked chicken, lime and sesame

Cook 300 g (10¹/₂ oz) **buckwheat noodles** in boiling water for 3 minutes. Rinse and drain really well, shaking out as much excess water as possible, and place into a bowl with 2 shredded **smoked chicken breasts**, 3–4 finely sliced **spring onions (scallions)**, 1 finely sliced Lebanese (short) **cucumber** and 2–3 handfuls **frisée**. Combine 1 tablespoon each **light soy sauce**, **black Chinese** or **balsamic vinegar**, **lime juice**, **sesame oil** and ¹/₂ teaspoon **sugar** in a bowl and stir until the sugar has dissolved. Pour over the salad ingredients, toss well to evenly coat the noodle salad in the dressing and serve sprinkled with a tablespoon of toasted **sesame seeds**.

tortillas are also used in a recipe on page...
45.

burritos and tortillas

three ways with

chilli bean burrito

Cook 1 chopped **onion** and
2 chopped **garlic cloves** in a frying
pan with a splash of sizzling **olive
oil** for 3–4 minutes, to soften the
onion. Add 1 teaspoon each **dried
oregano**, **ground cumin** and **chilli
flakes**, and stir for 1 minute. Add
500 g (1 lb 2 oz) **minced (ground)
beef** or **pork** and stir-fry for
8–10 minutes, to evenly brown.
Add 400 g (14 oz) tinned **kidney
beans** (drained, not rinsed, and
roughly mashed), 400 g (14 oz)
tinned **chopped tomatoes**, 125 ml
(4 fl oz/1/2 cup) water and a good
seasoning of **salt** and **black
pepper**. Boil the mixture then
rapidly simmer for 15 minutes,
stirring often. Meanwhile, wrap
4–6 **burritos** in foil and warm in
a 180°C (350°F/Gas 4) oven for
10 minutes. Serve the chilli beef
wrapped in the warm burritos with
some **sour cream** or **guacamole**
on the side.

artichoke, salami and olive tortilla

Have your oven hot and ready at
220°C (425°F/Gas 7). Place a large
tortilla on a baking tray. Spread
2 tablespoons **olive tapenade** over
the tortilla and top with 3 sliced
and drained **marinated artichokes**,
6–8 thin slices of **salami**, 1 sliced
tomato,150 g (51/2 oz/1 cup)
grated **mozzarella** and a good
grinding of **black pepper**. Place
another **tortilla** on top and cook in
the oven for 5 minutes. Turn over
and cook for a further 5 minutes,
or until golden. Cut each tortilla into
6–8 wedges and serve as a snack.

roasted vegetable, feta and mint quesadilla

Spread a couple of pieces of
grilled eggplant (aubergine) and
red capsicum (pepper) (both
available from the delicatessen
section at the supermarket)
over a **burrito**. Crumble over 75 g
(2 3/4 oz/1/2 cup) **feta**, 75 g (2 3/4 oz/
1/2 cup) grated **mozzarella** and
a handful of roughly torn **mint**.
Sprinkle over 1/2 teaspoon **chilli
flakes** and place another **burrito**
on top. Have a large non-stick
frying pan hot and almost
smoking. Add the quesadilla and
cook for 2 minutes. Flip over and
cook for a couple more minutes.
Remove to a chopping board and
cut into wedges. Serves 2.

butterbeans

three ways with

tapas butterbeans

Cut 3 ripe and tasty **tomatoes** in half and squeeze the juice and seeds into a bowl. Chop the tomatoes into bite-sized chunks. Heat 3 tablespoons **olive oil** in a frying pan and stir-fry the tomato pieces with 2 **garlic cloves** over a high heat for a few minutes to soften. Add 400 g (14 oz) tinned **butterbeans (lima beans)**, rinsed and drained, 2 teaspoons **tomato paste (concentrated purée)** and a small handful of torn **basil**. Season really well (both the beans and tomato like **salt** and **pepper**). Add the tomato juice and seeds to the pan and cook over a low heat for 5 minutes. Serve with some warm crunchy fresh **bread** as a shared starter.

creamy, garlicky bean dip

Put 400 g (14 oz) tinned **butterbeans (lima beans)**, rinsed and drained, in a saucepan with 3 tablespoons **pouring (whipping) cream**, 20 g (³/₄ oz) **butter** and 2 **garlic cloves**, and cook over a gentle heat for 5 minutes (don't let the mixture boil). Put the mixture in food processor and blend until smooth, thick and creamy. Add a splash of **milk** if too thick. Season well with **sea salt** and **black pepper**. Serve with fingers of toasted **Turkish (pide/flat) bread**.

tuscan butterbeans

Heat 2 tablespoons good **fruity olive oil** and 20 g (³/₄ oz) **butter** in a saucepan. When the butter starts to sizzle, add 2 chopped **garlic cloves** and 1 **bay leaf** and cook over a gentle heat for 2–3 minutes, to soften the garlic and flavour the oil. Add 400 g (14 oz) tinned **butterbeans (lima beans)**, rinsed and drained, a small handful of roughly chopped **black olives**, a handful of roughly chopped **flat-leaf (Italian) parsley** and a good grinding of **black pepper** to the pan. Cook for 5 minutes over a gentle heat and serve with **grilled lamb cutlets** or **fish**.

cannellini beans are also used in recipes on pages... 17 and 25.

cannellini beans

three ways with

really chunky white bean and pancetta soup

Cook 1 chopped carrot, 1 chopped onion, 1 chopped celery stalk and 40 g (1½ oz) chopped pancetta in a splash of olive oil for 2–3 minutes, until the vegetables are a little softened. Add 400 g (14 oz) tinned cannellini beans, rinsed and drained, 400 g (14 oz) tinned chopped tomatoes, 2 peeled and diced potatoes and 1.5 litres (52 fl oz/6 cups) chicken stock. Bring to the boil then reduce the heat to simmer for 30 minutes, until the potatoes are cooked through and the soup is really thick. Place a thick slice of bread in the bottom of a bowl and spoon over the chunky soup.

white bean and tuna salad

Whisk up 3 tablespoons good olive oil, 2 tablespoons red wine vinegar, 1 crushed garlic clove and 1 teaspoon dijon mustard in a bowl. In another bowl, toss together 400 g (14 oz) tinned cannellini beans, rinsed and drained, 1 chopped small red onion, 1 small handful black olives, 2–3 chopped anchovy fillets, 1 large handful each roughly chopped basil and flat-leaf (Italian) parsley and 225 g (8 oz) tinned tuna (with a little drizzle of the oil from the tin for extra flavour). Pour over the dressing, gently toss, being careful not to break up the tuna too much, and serve with warm bread as a starter.

smoky sausage and bean casserole

Heat a splash of light olive oil in a casserole dish and cook 1 chopped onion and 2 chopped smoked Italian sausages for a few minutes, so the onion softens and sizzles in the oil and the sausage starts to turn crisp around the edges. Add 400 g (14 oz) tinned cannellini beans, rinsed and drained, 400 g (14 oz) tinned tomatoes, 1 tablespoon soft brown sugar, 1 bay leaf, a few splashes of Tabasco and 125 ml (4 fl oz/½ cup) water. Bring to the boil then reduce the heat to a simmer for 15 minutes. Serve on its own or on toasted sourdough or Turkish (pide/flat) bread.

capers are also used in recipes on pages...
35, 43, 149, 183 and 187.

capers

three ways with

upside-down caper and tomato tart

Have your oven hot and ready at 220°C (425°F/Gas 7). Heat 2 tablespoons **olive oil** in an ovenproof frying pan. Add 1 tablespoon **salted small capers** (leave unrinsed as they will season the tart) and 1 teaspoon **rosemary leaves** and stir in the hot oil for 1 minute. Thickly slice 3 very ripe and tasty **tomatoes** and arrange the slices in a single layer on top of the capers and cook for 3–4 minutes, so the tomato softens. Lay a sheet of frozen **puff pastry** on top of the tomatoes, folding in the corners so it fits snugly in the pan. Bake for 15–20 minutes, until the pastry is puffed and golden. Remove and cool for a few minutes before carefully turning over onto a large plate. Add a good grinding of **black pepper** and enjoy with some **baby rocket (arugula) leaves** or a sprinkling of **goat's cheese feta**. Serves 2.

caper and herb sauce

Put 2 slices of **stale bread**, crusts removed, in a food processor with 2 tablespoons rinsed **capers**, 4–6 **anchovy fillets**, 1 teaspoon **dijon mustard**, a handful each of chopped **flat-leaf (Italian) parsley** and **mint** and a good squeeze of **lemon juice**. Blend to a paste and, with the motor running, slowly pour in 125 ml (4 fl oz/½ cup) good **olive oil**. Put in a bowl and season well. Use as a side for **grilled salmon**, toss through **green beans** or add to a **potato salad**.

tagliatelle with tuna and lemony capers

Cook 400 g (14 oz) **tagliatelle** or **fettucine** in boiling water for 8–10 minutes. Drain and return to the warm pan. Meanwhile, heat a generous splash of **olive oil** in a frying pan, add 2 tablespoons rinsed **capers** and fry for a few minutes. Add a generous squeeze of **lemon juice**, shake the pan around and put the capers in a bowl. Heat a few more splashes of **oil** in the pan and cook 2 chopped **garlic cloves** over a medium heat and add 3 tablespoons **small black olives** and 375 g (13 oz) tinned **tuna**, drained of oil. Stir for a few minutes to heat the tuna, being careful not to break it up too much. Add a handful of chopped **flat-leaf (Italian) parsley**, toss around gently and serve with the lemony capers on top and a good grinding of **black pepper**.

cashews are also used in a recipe on page...
47.

cashews

three ways with

cashew tabouleh in crisp lettuce

Put 130 g (4³/4 oz/³/4 cup) burghul (bulgur) in a dry saucepan and cook over a high heat for 2–3 minutes, shaking the pan constantly. Add 500 ml (17 fl oz/ 2 cups) water and 1 tablespoon olive oil to the pan and bring to the boil. Reduce the heat to really low, then place on a tight-fitting lid and cook for 15 minutes. Pour into a bowl and fluff with a fork. Add 2 handfuls flat-leaf (Italian) parsley, roughly chopped, 1 small handful mint, chopped, 1 finely chopped Lebanese (short) cucumber and 155 g (5¹/2 oz/ 1 cup) lightly toasted cashews. Whisk up 3 tablespoons each lemon juice and olive oil and stir well through the salad. Serve in crisp lettuce cups as a starter or as a side dish with lamb.

cashew and dill pesto

Blend 80 g (2³/4 oz/¹/2 cup) raw or dry-roasted cashews, 3 tablespoons roughly chopped dill, 1 handful flat-leaf (Italian) parsley, roughly chopped, 1 garlic clove, 3 tablespoons olive oil and a good squeeze of lemon juice in a food processor to form a rough paste, leaving little pieces of cashew intact. Remove and fold through 3 tablespoons grated parmesan. Serve on an antipasto platter, with roasted pumpkin (winter squash), goat's cheese or grilled fish.

grilled zucchini, cashew and feta salad

Slice 4 zucchini (courgettes) into 5 mm (¹/4 inch) strips and chargrill for 3–4 minutes each side. Put in a bowl with 1 small handful flat-leaf (Italian) parsley, chopped, 2 tablespoons chopped dill, 2 tablespoons olive oil, a good squeeze of lemon juice and salt and black pepper. Add 80 g (2³/4 oz/¹/2 cup) unsalted cashews to the bowl with 3 handfuls baby rocket (arugula) or baby English spinach leaves. Toss to combine and arrange on a serving plate. Crumble over 150 g (5¹/2 oz) soft feta and serve with some toasted ciabatta bread.

chicken stock is also used in recipes on pages...
15, 17, 21, 25, 27, 29, 33, 51, 55, 71, 75, 81, 89, 91, 93, 95,
103, 111, 117, 119, 123, 125, 127, 129, 131, 133, 135, 137, 145,
147, 155, 165, 169, 177, 185, 191, 193, 195, 199 and 211.

chicken stock

three ways with

chicken noodle soup

Cook 120 g (4¹/₄ oz) **angel hair pasta** or **egg vermicelli** in boiling water for 3–4 minutes and drain. Boil 1.5 litres (52 fl oz/6 cups) **chicken stock** and stir through 350 g (12 oz/2 cups) shredded meat and skin of a **barbecued chicken** and 1 large handful chopped **flat-leaf (Italian) parsley**. Add the pasta to the soup and cook for a couple of minutes to heat through. Season well and serve with thickly sliced **buttered toast**.

cajun corn chowder

Fry 1 chopped **onion** and 2 chopped **bacon slices** in 20 g (³/₄ oz) sizzling **butter** for 2–3 minutes. Add 400 g (14 oz/ 2 cups) **corn** (defrosted if frozen) 1 teaspoon **Cajun spice mix** and stir-fry for 2 minutes over a high heat. Add 750 ml (26 fl oz/3 cups) **chicken stock**, bring to the boil then simmer for 15 minutes. Blend the mixture in a food processor until smooth then return to the pan with 125 ml (4 fl oz/¹/₂ cup) **pouring (whipping) cream** and stir over a gentle heat for 2 minutes to heat through. Serve with a dollop of **sour cream** or **crème fraîche** on top.

cheat's chinese short soup

Bring 1 litre (35 fl oz/4 cups) **chicken stock** to the boil, add 1 tablespoon **light soy sauce** and 1 teaspoon **sesame oil** and simmer while cooking the dumplings. Cook 16 **ready-made Chinese won tons** or **soup dumplings** in boiling water for 2–3 minutes, until they rise to the top. Drain and place the dumplings in the bottom of 4 small soup bowls. Ladle over the hot stock and top each soup with some finely sliced **spring onions (scallions)** and a little extra drizzle of **sesame oil**.

chickpeas are also used in a recipe on page...
81.

chickpeas
three ways with

chickpea, smoky chorizo and bread salad

Place a **red capsicum (pepper)** in a really hot oven for 10 minutes until puffed up and darkened. Plunge into cold water for a minute then peel and finely slice the flesh and put into a bowl. Cook 2 sliced **chorizos** in a splash of sizzling **olive oil** for 2–3 minutes, so the chorizo sizzles and turns golden. Add the chorizo and any tasty oil from the pan to the capsicums with 400 g (14 oz) tinned **chickpeas**, rinsed and drained, 2 large handfuls **baby rocket (arugula) leaves** and 1 tablespoon **red wine vinegar**. Lightly toast 2 thick slices of **white bread**. Drizzle with a little **olive oil** and season well.

chickpea sesame dip

Blend 400 g (14 oz) tinned **chickpeas**, rinsed and drained, 2 **garlic cloves**, 125 g (4 1/2 oz/ 1/2 cup) **sour cream** or **crème fraîche**, 2 tablespoons **lemon juice** and 1 teaspoon **sesame oil** in a food processor until really smooth. Add a good amount of **sea salt** and **white pepper** to taste. Serve with a good pinch of **paprika** sprinkled on top and serve as you would with any dip or as a side to **grilled vegetables**.

italian chickpea soup

Heat a few splashes of **olive oil** in a saucepan and cook 1 chopped **onion**, 1 chopped **small fennel bulb**, 1 chopped **carrot**, 1 sliced **celery stalk**, 1 chopped **garlic clove** and 1 teaspoon chopped **rosemary** for 4–5 minutes in the sizzling oil, to soften the vegetables but not brown. Add 400 g (14 oz) tinned **chopped tomatoes**, 400 g (14 oz) tinned **chickpeas**, rinsed and drained, and 750 ml (26 fl oz/ 3 cups) **chicken** or **vegetable stock** and bring to the boil. Simmer for 15 minutes then stir through 3–4 handfuls roughly chopped **English spinach leaves**, and season really well. Simmer for 5 minutes, to wilt the spinach. Serve with warm **foccacia**.

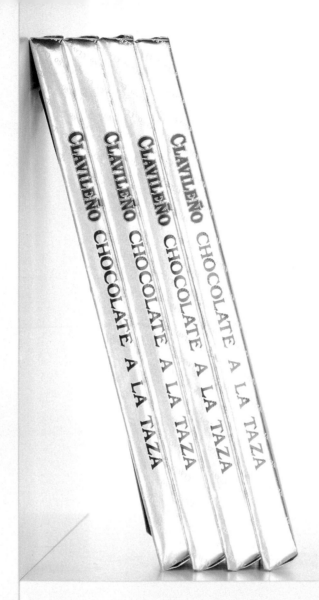

chocolate is also used in a recipe on page... 157.

chocolate

three ways with

chocolate pudding

Have your oven hot and ready at 180°C (350°F/Gas 4). Grease a 1 litre (35 fl oz/4 cup) baking dish. Put 200 g (7 oz) **dark chocolate** and 150 g (5¹/₂ oz) **butter** in a small saucepan over a gentle heat and stir until melted and smooth. Beat 3 **eggs** and 3 tablespoons **caster (superfine) sugar** for a minute. Beat in 60 g (2¹/₄ oz/ ¹/₂ cup) **self-raising flour** until there are no more lumps, then beat in the chocolate mix until smooth and evenly combined. Pour into the prepared dish. Quickly combine 375 ml (13 fl oz/ 1¹/₂ cups) boiling water with 3 tablespoons **soft brown sugar** and 2 tablespoons **unsweetened cocoa powder** in a jug and carefully pour over the pudding mixture. Bake for 40 minutes. The centre may still be soft and gooey like hot chocolate mousse. Enjoy with **vanilla ice cream**.

chocolate sauce

Heat 50 g (1³/₄ oz) **dark chocolate**, 125 ml (4 fl oz/¹/₂ cup) **thick (double/heavy) cream** and 1 tablespoon **soft brown sugar** in a small saucepan over a really gentle heat, stirring all the time until the mixture is totally smooth and all the chocolate has melted. This sauce can be served warm on **ice cream, sliced bananas** and **chopped nuts** and will keep well at room temperature for a few hours if made in advance.

over the top chocolate mousse

Put 200 g (7 oz) chopped **dark chocolate** and 3 tablespoons **strong coffee** in a bowl over a saucepan of gently simmering water for 8–10 minutes. Remove and beat for a minute, until totally smooth and glossy. Separate 3 **eggs** and beat the yolks, one at a time, into the chocolate until smooth. Stir through 60 g (2¹/₄ oz) melted **butter**. Beat the egg whites until they are softly peaking then fold into the chocolate mix. Beat 125 ml (4 fl oz/¹/₂ cup) **pouring (whipping) cream** to soft peaks, being careful not to overbeat (otherwise the mousse will be grainy). Fold the cream into the mousse, spoon into 4 individual glasses or cups, chill and enjoy.

chocolate / pantry

coconut milk is also used in recipes on pages...
121, 129, 169, 171 and 179.

coconut milk

three ways with

massaman curry

Cook 1 finely sliced **onion** in a splash of **vegetable oil** for 3–4 minutes. Add 2 tablespoons **soft brown sugar** and 2–3 tablespoons **massaman curry paste** to the pan and cook for 2 minutes. Add 600 ml (21 fl oz) **coconut milk** to the pan and bring to a gentle simmer. Add 2 peeled and quartered **large potatoes** and 3 tablespoons **unsalted raw peanuts** to the pan and cook for 15 minutes. Cut 2 **lamb loin fillets** into small bite-sized pieces and add to the pan, cover and cook for 10 minutes. Stir through 1 tablespoon **fish sauce** and a handful of **basil** and serve with **rice**. For an ideal garnish, top with some **crisp-fried Asian shallots** and some extra **basil**.

potato and tomato curry

Heat a splash of **oil** in a frying pan and stir-fry 1 sliced **red onion** and 8 unpeeled **baby potatoes** for 4–5 minutes, shaking the pan around so the onions soften and sizzle. Add 2 tablespoons **mild Indian curry paste** (try a balti or madras) and stir-fry for 2–3 minutes, to bring out all the hidden spices in the paste. Add 250 ml (9 fl oz/1 cup) water, bring to the boil and cover with a tight-fitting lid. Cook over a low heat for 15 minutes, stirring often, so the potatoes soften a little. Add 400 ml (14 fl oz) **coconut milk** and 250 g (9 oz) **cherry tomatoes** and bring to a simmer. Cook for 5 minutes, so the tomatoes just begin to split, stir through 1 handful **coriander (cilantro) leaves**, chopped, and serve with some **minted plain yoghurt** and **rice**.

easy prawn curry

Heat a splash of **vegetable oil** in a pan. Stir-fry 12–16 **raw large prawns (shrimp)**, peeled and deveined, in the sizzling oil for 2–3 minutes, until they curl up and turn pink. Add 1 chopped **onion** and 1 tablespoon **madras curry powder** and stir-fry for 2–3 minutes, to release all the hidden spices in the powder. Add 400 ml (14 fl oz) **coconut milk**, bring to the boil and reduce the heat to simmer for 10 minutes. Add 65 g (2 1/4 oz/ 1/2 cup) **peas** (defrosted if frozen) and 40 g (1 1/2 oz) **butter**, cook over a gentle heat for 2 minutes and serve with **rice**.

couscous is also used in a recipe on page...
201.

couscous

three ways with

honey pumpkin couscous salad

Have your oven hot and ready at 180°C (350°F/Gas 4). Place 600 g (1 lb 5 oz/4 cups) peeled and chopped bite-sized pieces of pumpkin (winter squash) in a bowl with 1 sliced red onion, 2 tablespoons honey and a good splash of olive oil. Toss around to evenly combine, place on a baking tray and roast for 30 minutes. Meanwhile, place 185 g (6½ oz/ 1 cup) couscous and 20 g (¾ oz) butter in a bowl. Pour over 250 ml (9 fl oz/1 cup) boiling water and cover tightly for 10 minutes. Fluff once or twice then cover again for 5 minutes. Place the couscous in a bowl and fluff and separate with your fingers. Add the roasted pumpkin mixture to the couscous with 3 tablespoons toasted flaked almonds, toss around and enjoy as a warm salad or as a side to grilled lamb.

smoky spiced couscous

Place 280 g (10 oz/1½ cups) couscous, 1 teaspoon ground cumin and ½ teaspoon each ground coriander, chilli powder and paprika in a dry saucepan. Shake the pan over a medium heat for 2–3 minutes, to release the aromas in the spices, being careful not to burn the couscous. Turn the heat off and pour 375 ml (13 fl oz/1½ cups) boiling water into the pan. Add 40 g (1½ oz) butter, stir quickly and cover the pan tightly for 10 minutes. Fluff with a fork and return the lid for 2 minutes. Serve as you would with any couscous; its intense flavour goes really well with simply grilled meats and fish, chargrilled vegetables and yoghurt.

seafood and couscous stew

Heat a splash of olive oil in a frying pan and cook 1 chopped onion and 2 chopped garlic cloves for a few minutes until softened. Add 750 ml (26 fl oz/3 cups) chicken or fish stock, 400 g (14 oz) tinned chopped tomatoes, 3 tablespoons couscous, a generous pinch of saffron and ½ teaspoon paprika to the pan and bring to the boil. Simmer for 8–10 minutes then add 400 g (14 oz) white fish fillets, cut into chunks, and 12 peeled and deveined raw prawns (shrimp). Cook over a gentle simmer for 10 minutes, until the fish is white and the prawns are pink and curled. Serve with a handful of flat-leaf (Italian) parsley, roughly chopped, and lemon wedges on the side.

curry powder is also used in recipes on pages...
71, 81, 115 and 177.

curry powder

three ways with

chicken curry

Have your oven hot and ready at 180°C (350°F/Gas 4). Cut a **whole chicken** into 10–12 pieces. Combine 3 tablespoons **plain (all-purpose) flour** and 3 tablespoons **curry powder** in a bowl and toss the chicken pieces around in the mix to coat all over. Heat a few splashes of **vegetable oil** in a heavy-based casserole dish and cook the chicken in batches for 3–4 minutes, turning often, so they sizzle and turn golden in the oil. Pour off all but 1 tablespoon of oil from the pot and stir 1 chopped **onion** and 2 chopped **garlic cloves** in the spicy oil for 2–3 minutes, so the onion sizzles and turns golden. Return the chicken to the pan with 500 ml (17 fl oz/2 cups) **chicken stock** and 1 chopped **carrot**. Bring to the boil and cook in the oven, uncovered, for 50 minutes. Stir through 130 g (4³/4 oz/1 cup) **peas** (defrosted if using frozen) and return to the oven for 10 minutes. Serve with **rice** and warm **naan bread**.

spiced tomato and lentil soup

Cook 1 chopped **onion**, 2 chopped **garlic cloves**, 1 teaspoon chopped **ginger** and 1 tablespoon **mild curry powder** in 40 g (1¹/2 oz) sizzling **butter** for 3–4 minutes, to release all the hidden spices in the powder. Add 125 g (4¹/2 oz/¹/2 cup) **red** or **brown lentils**, 400 g (14 oz) tinned **tomatoes** and 2 litres (70 fl oz/8 cups) water. Bring to the boil and cook on a rapid simmer for 40–45 minutes so the lentils are soft, almost mushy, and you have a thick soup.

curried beef shepherd's pie

Have your oven hot and ready at 180°C (350°F/Gas 4). Cook 4 peeled and chopped **large all-purpose potatoes** in boiling water until soft. Drain and mash until really smooth with 3 tablespoons **milk**. Set aside. Cook 1 chopped **onion** and 1 chopped **carrot** in 40 g (1¹/2 oz) sizzling **butter** for 2–3 minutes. Add 2–3 tablespoons **mild curry powder** and stir-fry for 1 minute, to release all the hidden spices. Add 500 g (1 lb 2 oz) **minced (ground) beef** and stir-fry for 5–6 minutes, to evenly brown, breaking up any large chunks. Add 250 ml (9 fl oz/1 cup) water and boil rapidly for 5 minutes, until almost all the liquid has gone. Stir through 155 g (5¹/2 oz/1 cup) **peas** (defrosted if using frozen). Spoon into a ovenproof dish, top with the potato and cook in the oven for 30 minutes.

curry powder / pantry

desiccated coconut is also used in recipes on pages...
141 and 163.

desiccated coconut

three ways with

coconut and curry leaf rice

Cook 200 g (7 oz/1 cup) long-grain rice (try basmati) in 1 litre (35 fl oz/4 cups) boiling water for 20 minutes. Drain well. Heat a few splashes of vegetable oil in a saucepan and cook 1 sliced green chilli, 1 teaspoon black or yellow mustard seeds and 6–8 curry leaves until the mustard seeds start to sizzle and pop. Add 3 tablespoons desiccated coconut and stir-fry for 3–4 minutes, until the coconut starts to turn golden. Remove from the heat and stir through the rice and a small handful of chopped coriander (cilantro) leaves.

coconut prawns

Peel and devein 12 raw large prawns (shrimp), but leave the tail on for perfect finger food. Put 60 g (2¼ oz/½ cup) plain (all-purpose) flour in a bowl, 2 beaten eggs in another small bowl and 90 g (3¼ oz/1 cup) desiccated coconut in a third bowl. Dip the prawns, one at a time, first in the flour, then the egg and, finally, in the coconut. Press down firmly so the prawns are covered all over with the coconut. Heat a saucepan one-third full of vegetable oil over a medium heat until the surface of the oil is shimmering. Cook the prawns in two batches, for 3–4 minutes. Drain on paper towel and serve with your favourite sweet chilli or chilli sauce.

coconut and makrut leaf chicken curry

Chop 3 skinless, boneless chicken breasts into large bite-sized pieces. Put 45 g (1½ oz/½ cup) desiccated coconut in a saucepan and stir-fry over a medium heat until the coconut turns nicely golden. Remove from the pan. Heat a splash of vegetable oil in the saucepan and stir-fry 2 tablespoons yellow curry paste in the oil for 2–3 minutes, to release the hidden spices in the paste. Add 4–6 makrut (kaffir lime) leaves, 2 teaspoons soft brown sugar and the chicken to the pan, stir-frying for 5 minutes, until the chicken is golden all over. Add 400 ml (14 fl oz) coconut milk to the pan, bring to the boil then simmer on a low heat for 10 minutes, to gently poach the chicken. Stir through the coconut and serve with rice.

dried apricots

three ways with

moroccan chicken with apricots

Chop a **chicken** into 8–10 pieces. Toss the chicken pieces in a bowl with 1 teaspoon **ground cumin**, 1 teaspoon **ground coriander** and a generous seasoning of **salt** and **black pepper**. Heat a few splashes of **light cooking oil** in a large, heavy-based saucepan and cook the chicken pieces in batches for a few minutes each side, until well browned. Return all the chicken to the pan with 180 g (6½ oz/1 cup) **dried apricots**, 6–8 **pitted dates**, 500 ml (17 fl oz/2 cups) **chicken stock** and 3 tablespoons **honey**. Bring to the boil then reduce the heat to low, cover and simmer for 40 minutes, stirring now and then. Stir through 1 large handful **coriander (cilantro) leaves**, roughly chopped, and serve with **couscous**.

smoked chicken, apricot and feta salad

Finely shred 2 **smoked chicken breasts** and put in a bowl with 3 tablespoons chopped **dried apricots**, 1 large handful **flat-leaf (Italian) parsley**, 80 g (2¾ oz/ ½ cup) toasted **almonds** and 2 large handfuls picked **watercress**. Crumble over 75 g (2½ oz) **marinated feta** (or a mild Danish feta) and gently toss with 2 tablespoons good **olive oil**, 1 tablespoon **red wine vinegar** and a good seasoning of **salt** and **black pepper**.

tipsy apricots with pistachio yoghurt and honey

Put 180 g (6½ oz/1 cup) **dried apricots**, 2 tablespoons **caster (superfine) sugar**, 375 ml (13 fl oz/1½ cups) water and 125 ml (4 fl oz/½ cup) **white wine** in a saucepan and bring to the boil. Reduce the heat to really low and cover with a tight-fitting lid for 20 minutes. Turn off the heat and allow to sit and soften in the pan until cool. Beat 125 g (4½ oz/ ½ cup) **Greek-style yoghurt** with 3 tablespoons chopped **pistachios**. Serve the stewed apricots with the yoghurt and a good drizzling of **honey** all over.

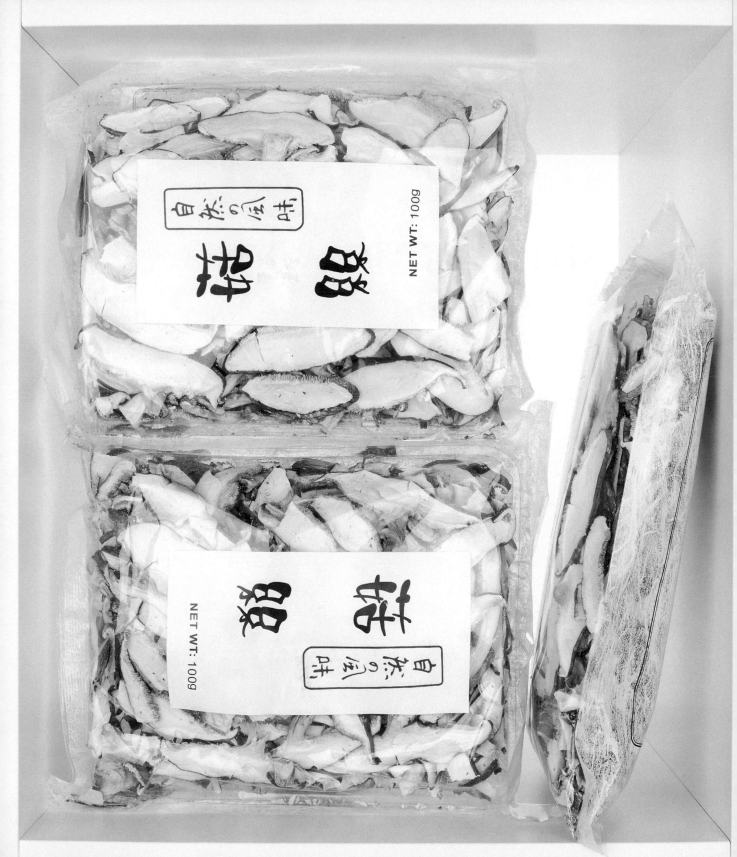

dried mushrooms are also used in a recipe on page...
165.

dried mushrooms

three ways with

hot and sour mushroom soup

Soak 6 **dried mushrooms** in 250 ml (9 fl oz/1 cup) boiling water for 15 minutes. Reserve the liquid, remove the stems and slice the caps. Put the mushroom soaking liquid in a saucepan with 1 litre (35 fl oz/4 cups) **chicken stock**, 3 tablespoons **Chinese black vinegar**, 1 tablespoon **light soy sauce**,1 teaspoon **black pepper**, 140 g (5 oz) tinned and drained **bamboo shoots**, 2 handfuls stemmed and sliced **button mushrooms** and 1 tablespoon **cornflour (cornstarch)**. Gradually bring the soup to the boil, stirring constantly until it thickens slightly. Add the mushrooms and allow to simmer for a few minutes before serving.

simmered mushrooms with tofu

Put 8 **dried mushrooms** in a bowl and cover with boiling water for 20 minutes. Cut off and discard the stems and cut any larger caps in half. Put the caps in a saucepan with 125 ml (4 fl oz/1/2 cup) of the soaking liquid, 500 ml (17 fl oz/ 2 cups) water, 2–3 thick slices of **ginger**, 2 tablespoons **light soy sauce**, 2 tablespoons **oyster sauce** and a good pinch of **sugar**. Bring to the boil then reduce the heat and simmer for 15 minutes. Add 185 g (6½ oz/1 cup) cubed **firm tofu** and cook for a further 5 minutes. Serve with **rice** and **steamed Chinese greens**.

stir-fried mushrooms with chinese cabbage

Put 6–8 **dried mushrooms** in a bowl and cover with boiling water for 20 minutes. Discard the mushroom stems and reserve 2 tablespoons of the soaking liquid. Cut the caps in half. Heat 2 tablespoons **vegetable oil** in a hot wok and stir-fry 1 tablespoon grated **ginger**, 2 chopped **garlic cloves** and 2 chopped **spring onions (scallions)** for a few seconds to flavour the oil. Add the mushrooms and 110 g (3¾ oz) tinned **bamboo shoots**, well drained, and stir-fry for 1 minute. Add 135 g (4¾ oz/3 cups) sliced **Chinese cabbage** and stir-fry for 2 minutes, until the cabbage has softened, then add the mushroom liquid and 2 tablespoons **light soy sauce** to the wok. Stir-fry for 1 minute and served drizzled with some **sesame oil**.

fish sauce is also used in recipes on pages...
75, 95, 115, 129, 155, 169, 171, 179, 199 and 213.

fish sauce

three ways with

sweet and sour herbed eggplant salad

Have your oven hot and ready at 220°C (425°F/Gas 7). Combine 2 tablespoons **fish sauce**, 3 tablespoons **lemon juice**, ¼ teaspoon **chilli powder** and 2 teaspoons **sugar** in a small bowl and stir to dissolve the sugar. Prick the skin of a large **eggplant (aubergine)** all over with a fork. Place the eggplant directly onto the middle rack in the oven for 10–15 minutes, so the skin is puffed and burnt. Plunge into cold water for a few minutes. Peel off the skin, tear the flesh into long pieces and place in a bowl with 1 small handful each **coriander (cilantro) leaves**, **mint** and **basil**, and 1 finely sliced **red onion**. Pour over the dressing and gently toss the ingredients to combine all the flavours.

caramel chicken

Cut 4 **chicken leg quarters** to separate the legs from the thighs. Heat a splash of **vegetable oil** in a casserole dish and cook the chicken pieces (you may need to do this in batches) for 3–4 minutes each side so the skin crisps to golden. Drain the oil, then return all the chicken to the pan and add 3 tablespoons **fish sauce**, 3 tablespoons **sugar**, 3 crushed **garlic cloves**, ½ teaspoon **white pepper**, 1 tablespoon **dark soy sauce** and 500 ml (17 fl oz/2 cups) water, and bring to the boil. Reduce the heat to a gentle simmer for 45–50 minutes, stirring often until almost all the liquid has gone and the sauce thickly coats the chicken.

sweet pork larb in baby cos

Heat 2 tablespoons **vegetable oil** in a hot wok and stir-fry 3 chopped **garlic cloves** and 4 finely chopped **spring onions (scallions)** for 2 minutes, until crisp and golden. Add 3 tablespoons **sugar** and stir-fry for a minute so it dissolves, then quickly add 250 ml (9 fl oz/1 cup) **chicken stock** (it will sizzle here), 2 tablespoons **fish sauce**, ½ teaspoon **chilli powder** and 300 g (10½ oz) **minced (ground) pork**. Stir-fry over a high heat for 8–10 minutes, until the liquid has almost gone and the pork is quite dark. Spoon the sweet pork into crisp **baby cos (romaine) lettuce leaves** and serve as a starter with a **coriander (cilantro) sprig** and **lime wedges** to squeeze over.

green curry paste

three ways with

crispy skinned fish in jungle curry

Rub a little **sea salt** and **white pepper** on the skin of 4 **white fish fillets**. Heat a splash of **vegetable oil** in a wok and stir-fry 1 finely chopped **onion** and 2 finely chopped **garlic cloves** for 2 minutes, to soften the onion. Add 2 tablespoons **green curry paste** and a good pinch of **sugar** to the pan and cook for a minute or so, releasing all the hidden spices (that will almost make you want to sneeze). Add 375 ml (13 fl oz/1½ cups) **chicken stock**, 4–6 **makrut (kaffir lime) leaves** and 1 tablespoon **fish sauce** to the pan and gently simmer while you cook the fish. Heat a few tablespoons of **vegetable oil** in a non-stick frying pan. When smoking hot, add the fish pieces, skin side down, and cook for 3 4 minutes, gently pressing down with a spatula. Turn over and cook for 2–3 minutes. Put into a bowl and spoon over the hot jungle sauce with some extra finely shredded **makrut leaves** on top.

spicy lime and peanut chicken

Whiz-up 3 tablespoons **peanuts** in a food processor until finely chopped. Put in a bowl with 2 tablespoons **green curry paste**, 1 tablespoon **soft brown sugar** and a few splashes of **fish sauce** and **black pepper** for seasoning. Add 4 sliced **chicken thigh fillets**, tossing around to really coat in the spice mix. Heat a good few splashes of **vegetable oil** in a wok or frying pan. When smoking hot, add the chicken and stir-fry for about 8 minutes so the chicken pieces really crisp up. Drain any excess oil from the pan. Add 2 tablespoons **lime juice** and 3 tablespoons **chicken stock** to the pan and stir-fry for a few minutes, until almost all the stock has evaporated. Serve topped with freshly ground **black pepper** and a handful of chopped **coriander (cilantro) leaves**.

green curry with salmon and aromatic herbs

Spoon a few tablespoons of the solidified cream from the top of a 400 ml (14 fl oz) tin of **coconut milk** into a saucepan and boil. When it is really bubbling, add 2 tablespoons **green curry paste** and stir-fry for 2–3 minutes to release all the hidden aromatic spices in the paste. Add 2 teaspoons **sugar** to the pan and cook for a minute then add the remaining coconut milk and 6–8 **makrut (kaffir lime) leaves**. Bring to a gentle simmer then add 400 g (14 oz) bite-sized cubes of **salmon fillet**. Cover with a lid and cook for 5–6 minutes, to gently poach the salmon. Remove from the heat and stir though 1 small handful **Thai basil** and 1 tablespoon each **fish sauce** and **lime juice**.

green curry paste / pantry

green lentils

three ways with

slow-cooked lamb shanks with lentils

Have your oven hot and ready at 160°C (315°F/Gas 2–3). Put 4 lamb shanks, 40 g (1¹/₂ oz) chopped pancetta, 400 g (14 oz) tinned chopped tomatoes, 500 ml (17 fl oz/2 cups) beef or chicken stock, 250 ml (9 fl oz/1 cup) red wine, 100 g (3¹/₂ oz/¹/₂ cup) green (puy) lentils and 2 bay leaves in a casserole dish, season well and cover with a tight-fitting lid. Cook in the oven for 2¹/₂ hours, turning the shanks after 1¹/₂ hours.

roasted lamb rack with marinated feta and lentils

Have your oven hot and ready at 180°C (350°F/Gas 4). Combine 100 g (3¹/₄ oz/¹/₂ cup) green (puy) lentils in the bottom of a roasting pan with 1 chopped carrot, 1 chopped onion, 1 sliced celery stalk, 2 chopped garlic cloves and 500 ml (17 fl oz/2 cups) beef stock. Cook for 30 minutes then remove from the oven. Rub 75 g (2¹/₂ oz/¹/₂ cup) marinated feta over 2 racks of lamb (6-cutlet). Sit the lamb on the lentils, grind over some black pepper and drizzle with 1 tablespoon of the tasty oil from the feta and cook in the oven for a further 20 minutes, until the cheese crust on the lamb is cooked golden. Allow the lamb to rest for 5 minutes before cutting and serving with the lentils.

lentil, chorizo and goat's cheese salad

Cook 200 g (7 oz/1 cup) green (puy) lentils in boiling water for 30 minutes. Meanwhile, cook 2 thinly sliced chorizos with a splash of olive oil in a hot pan for 4–5 minutes, stirring so the pieces cook to an even golden. Put the pieces and any of the tasty oil from the pan in a large bowl with 3 handfuls mixed salad leaf, 120 g (4¹/₄ oz/1 cup) crumbled soft goat's cheese and the lentils. Mix up 2 tablespoons good olive oil, 2 tablespoons red wine vinegar and 1 teaspoon dijon mustard in a bowl and pour over the salad. Toss around to evenly combine the ingredients.

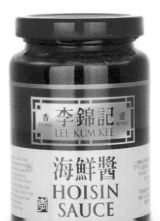

hoisin sauce is also used in a recipe on page... 169.

hoisin sauce

three ways with

chinese barbecued pork

Toss 2 **pork loin fillets** in a bowl with 3 tablespoons **hoisin sauce**, 1 teaspoon **sesame oil**, 1 tablespoon **light soy sauce** and 1 tablespoon **soft brown sugar**, making sure the marinade is all over the meat. Leave for 30 minutes (or overnight in the refrigerator if you have the time). Have your oven hot and ready at 180°C (350°F/Gas 4). Place the pork on a rack over a baking tray. Pour 250 ml (9 fl oz/1 cup) water into the bottom of the tray and cook in the oven for 40 minutes, turning after 20 minutes. Allow to rest before serving warm with **steamed Chinese greens** or allow to cool and serve wrapped in little **Peking-duck-style pancakes** with sliced **cucumber** and **spring onion (scallion)**.

mongolian lamb cutlets

Put 12 **lamb cutlets** in a bowl with 125 ml (4 fl oz/½ cup) **hoisin sauce**, tossing them around to coat in the sauce. Heat a good few splashes of **vegetable oil** and ½ teaspoon **sesame oil** in a hot frying pan and cook the cutlets in batches for 1 minute each side. Remove the cutlets and cook 2 sliced **onions** for 6–8 minutes on a gentle heat, until really soft and well browned. Add 1 chopped **garlic clove** and 1 teaspoon grated **ginger** and cook for a minute to flavour the onions. Return the cutlets to the pan with 125 ml (4 fl oz/½ cup) **chicken stock** and 1 tablespoon **light soy sauce**. Let the liquid boil for 2–3 minutes, turning the cutlets in the boiling sauce, so they are glazed and coated in the sauce. Serve with **green beans** or **pumpkin (winter squash) mash**.

eggplant in chilli hoisin

Cut 1 **large eggplant (aubergine)** into 3 cm (1¼ inch) pieces. Heat 3 tablespoons **vegetable oil** in a wok or frying pan. When the surface is shimmering, add the eggplant pieces and fry for 3–4 minutes, until golden. Remove and place on paper towel. Drain all but 1 teaspoon of oil from the pan and stir-fry 2 seeded and chopped **small red chillies**, 1 chopped **garlic clove**, 2 finely chopped **spring onions (scallions)** and 2 teaspoons grated **ginger** for a few seconds. Add 2 tablespoons **hoisin sauce**, 3 tablespoons **chicken stock** and a good pinch of **sugar** to the pan and boil for 2–3 minutes, until thickened slightly. Return the eggplant to the pan, gently toss through the sauce and serve with **rice** and **steamed Chinese greens**.

hoisin sauce / *pantry*

honey is also used in recipes on pages... 117, 123, 163 and 213.

honey

three ways with

tofu with honey and black pepper

Heat 1 tablespoon **vegetable oil** in a saucepan on a high heat and cook 1 chopped **garlic clove** and 1 teaspoon grated **ginger** for a few seconds. Add 125 ml (4 fl oz/^{1}/$_2$ cup) **chicken stock**, 3 tablespoons **honey** and 1 teaspoon **black pepper** to the pan and boil for 4–5 minutes, until the mixture is syrupy. Cut a 600 g (1 lb 5 oz) block of **soft (silken) tofu** into 2–3 cm (^{3}/$_4$–1^1/$_4$ inch) cubes. Put the pieces on some paper towel to drain while you heat the oil to fry in. Heat 250 ml (9 fl oz/1 cup) **vegetable oil** in a wok. When the surface of the oil shimmers, dip half of the tofu in some **cornflour (cornstarch)**, shake off the excess and fry for 1–2 minutes, until nicely golden. Reheat to cook the remaining tofu. Put the cooked tofu on a plate, warm the honey sauce and pour over.

honey-and-spice lamb cutlets

Have your oven hot and ready at 220°C (425°F/Gas 7). Mix 3 tablespoons **honey**, 1 tablespoon **light soy sauce**, 1 tablespoon **lemon juice** and ^{1}/$_2$ teaspoon **five-spice** in a bowl. Add 12 **lamb cutlets** and toss to coat evenly in the honey mixture. Heat a splash of **vegetable oil** in a non-stick frying pan over a medium–high heat. Cook the cutlets in batches for 1 minute each side (you may need to wipe the pan clean between batches), transfer to a baking tray and cook in the oven for 5 minutes (for medium–rare). Serve with **pumpkin (winter squash) mash** or **steamed greens**.

honey prawns

Heat 175 g (6 oz/^{1}/$_2$ cup) **honey** in a saucepan over a gentle heat until runny, and set aside. Heat 250 ml (9 fl oz/1 cup) **vegetable oil** in a wok. Combine 125 g (4^1/$_2$ oz/ 1 cup) **tempura flour** (available in the Asian section at supermarkets) with 250 ml (9 fl oz/1 cup) ice cold water until just combined but still a little lumpy. Dip 12 **raw large prawns (shrimp)**, 2 at a time, in the batter. Shake off excess batter and cook in the hot oil for 2–3 minutes and remove to a plate. Repeat with the remaining prawns. Quickly reheat the honey, pour over the prawns and sprinkle over 1 tablespoon lightly toasted **sesame seeds**.

hot pepper sauce is also used in recipes on pages...
63 and 103.

hot pepper sauce

three ways with

spicy tomato rice

Blend 400 g (14 oz) tinned tomatoes, 1 chopped onion, 2 chopped garlic cloves and 1–2 teaspoons Tabasco (or another hot pepper sauce) in a food processor until smooth. Heat 2 tablespoons light olive oil in a saucepan and stir-fry 400 g (14 oz/2 cups) long-grain rice in the oil for 3–4 minutes. Add the tomato mixture and 750 ml (26 fl oz/3 cups) chicken stock and bring to the boil. Cover with a lid and reduce the heat to really low for 25 minutes. Remove from the heat and stir through 155 g (5½ oz/1 cup) peas (defrosted if using frozen). Place the lid on for a further 5 minutes. Fluff the rice with a fork and stir through 1 large handful coriander (cilantro) leaves, roughly chopped. Season with salt and black pepper and serve.

tabasco mayonnaise

Put 3 egg yolks in a food processor with 2 teaspoons Tabasco (or another hot pepper sauce) and 1 teaspoon sea salt, and blend for a few seconds. With the motor running very slowly, add 250 ml (9 fl oz/1 cup) light olive oil, starting with a few drops at a time then gradually in a steady stream, until all the oil is incorporated and the mayonnaise is thick and creamy. You may add a squeeze of lime juice and a handful of coriander (cilantro) leaves, finely chopped. Enjoy as a dip for wedges, chargrilled chicken or a spicy addition to potato salad.

mexican baked beans

Cook 1 chopped onion, 2 chopped bacon slices and 1 sliced small red capsicum (pepper) in a splash of hot vegetable oil for 3–4 minutes, to soften the vegetables and crisp the bacon. Add 800 g (1 lb 12 oz) tinned baked beans and 1–2 teaspoons Tabasco (or another hot pepper sauce). Bring to the boil and simmer for 10 minutes, until the sauce has thickened. Serve at a picnic or with barbecued sausages.

hot pepper sauce / pantry

indian curry paste is also used in recipes on pages...
81, 115, 147, 205 and 215.

indian curry paste

spinach and cheese curry

Cook 280 g (10 oz/2 cups) cubed **paneer** in a splash of sizzling **vegetable oil** in a non-stick frying pan for 2–3 minutes, until light golden. Remove to a plate and pour off any excess oil from the pan. Heat 40 g (1½ oz) **butter** in the pan and, when it is sizzles, add 2 tablespoons **mild Indian curry paste** (try madras or balti) and stir-fry for 2 minutes, to bring out all the hidden spices. Add 1 kg (2 lb 4 oz/2 bunches) roughly chopped **English spinach** to the pan and stir-fry for 3–4 minutes, until the spinach has totally wilted. Add 250 ml (9 fl oz/1 cup) **pouring (whipping) cream** to the pan, stirring to combine. Put the mixture in food processor and blend to a smooth paste. Return the sauce to the pan, add the cheese and heat gently for 2 minutes. Serve with **basmati rice**.

curry roast chicken

Have your oven hot and ready at 180°C (350°F/Gas 4) and put a baking tray to heat in the oven. Combine 60 g (2¼ oz) softened **butter** with 2–3 tablespoons **mild Indian curry paste** (try madras). Wash and pat dry a **chicken**. Squeeze a **lemon** over the chicken and rub the juice into the skin. Rub half of the curry butter under the skin, between the skin and the breast meat, and smear the remaining butter all over the chicken. Place on the hot tray and roast for 1 hour and 10 minutes. Serve with **couscous**, **tomato and onion raita**, **mango chutney** and **minted yoghurt**.

madras rack of lamb

Have your oven hot and ready at 220°C (425°F/Gas 7) and put a baking tray to heat in the oven. Blend 3 tablespoons **madras curry paste** (or another mild Indian curry paste), 125 g (4½ oz/½ cup) **plain yoghurt** and 1 large handful **coriander (cilantro) leaves** in a food processor to make a smooth, spiced and tangy paste. Rub the paste over 2 **racks of lamb (6-cutlet)** and spinkle over 1 teaspoon **sea salt** and lots of **black pepper**. Place the racks on the hot tray and into the oven for 20 minutes for pink lamb, 5 minutes more for medium. Remove from the oven and wrap in foil for 5 minutes before cutting into individual cutlets. Squeeze over some **lemon juice** and serve as individual pieces or 3–4 cutlets each as a meal.

jam is also used in recipes on pages...
227 and 209.

jam

three ways with

jam cake

Have your oven hot and ready at 180°C (350°F/Gas 4). Grease a 25 cm (10 inch) bundt cake tin. Put 185 g (6¹/₂ oz) softened **butter** and 185 g (6¹/₂ oz/1 cup) **soft brown sugar** in a food processor and blend until smooth. Add 3 **eggs**, one at a time, and blend for a few seconds between each addition. Add 250 g (9 oz/1 cup) **sour cream** or **crème fraîche** and 250 g (9 oz/2 cups) **self-raising flour** to the food processor and blend until you have a thick batter. Stir through 315 g (11 oz/1 cup) **jam**, spoon into the tin and bake for 45 minutes. Serve warm with **ice cream** or **custard**.

raspberry and croissant puddings

Have your oven hot and ready at 220°C (425°F/Gas 7). Grease 4 250 ml (9 fl oz/1 cup) ovenproof dishes. Cut 2 small **croissants** crossways into thin slices and spread a little **raspberry jam** on one side of each slice. Divide the slices between the dishes, placing in layers. Put 300 ml (10¹/₂ fl oz) **pouring (whipping) cream**, 100 ml (3¹/₂ fl oz) **milk** and 2 tablespoons **custard powder** in a small saucepan and whisk over a gentle heat for a few minutes, until slightly thickened. Pour the custard mix over the croissant slices and bake for 15 minutes, until the edges are golden and look set. The custard may still be deliciously soft underneath. Allow to cool a little before serving.

hot jam and coconut tarts

Have your oven hot and ready at 220°C (425°F/Gas 7) and place a baking tray in the oven. Place 4 **mini sweet tart cases** (try Pampas, leaving the pastry in the foil case) on the hot tray and bake for 8–10 minutes, until the crimped edges of the tart shell turn golden. Remove and put 1 tablespoon **jam** (any berry flavour works best) and a sprinkling of **desiccated coconut** on top and return to the oven for 4–5 minutes, until the coconut turns golden. Allow to cool a little then serve with some **whipped cream** or **vanilla ice cream**.

kidney beans are also used in a recipe on page...
99.

kidney beans

three ways with

spiced potato and bean salad

Cook 2 peeled and cubed **potatoes** in boiling water for 10 minutes. Drain well. Heat 2 tablespoons **vegetable oil** in a frying pan and cook 2 finely sliced **red onions** and 1 chopped **large green chilli** for 3–4 minutes, to soften the onions. Add the potatoes to the pan with 1 teaspoon **sea salt** and 1 teaspoon **ground cumin**. Stir-fry for 4–5 minutes. Put the spiced potatoes in a bowl with 400 g (14 oz) tinned **kidney beans**, rinsed and drained, 1 tablespoon **lemon juice**, a good grinding of **black pepper** and a large handful of **coriander (cilantro) leaves**. Toss to combine and serve.

indian kidney bean curry

Cook 1 chopped **onion** and 1 chopped **garlic clove** in a splash of **vegetable oil** for 2–3 minutes, so the onion softens. Add 1/2 teaspoon each **ground cumin** and **chilli powder** and stir-fry for a minute. Add 400 g (14 oz) tinned **tomatoes** and 500 ml (17 fl oz/ 2 cups) water and boil for 10 minutes. Add 400 g (14 oz) tinned **kidney beans**, rinsed and drained, and a handful of **coriander (cilantro) leaves** and simmer for 5 minutes. Serve with **basmati rice**, **poppadoms** and **cucumber** slices.

smoky bean nachos

Cook 300 g (10 1/2 oz) finely chopped **smoked pork sausage** and 1 chopped **onion** in a splash of sizzling **olive oil** for 4–5 minutes, so the sausage starts to turn golden. Add 1 teaspoon **dried thyme**, 400 g (14 oz) tinned **kidney beans**, rinsed and drained, 400 g (14 oz) tinned **chopped tomatoes**, 125 ml (4 fl oz/ 1/2 cup) water and boil for 5 minutes, until thickened. Season well with **salt** and **black pepper**. Serve over warmed **corn chips** or wrapped in **tortilla** with grated **cheddar** and **guacamole** or **sour cream** on the side.

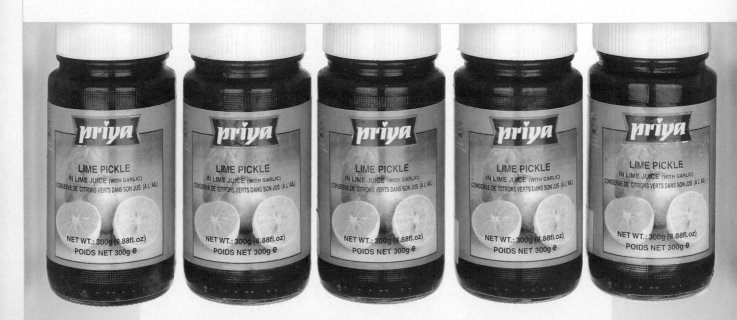

lime pickle

three ways with

lime pickle, coriander and soy swordfish

Put 4 tablespoons **lime pickle** in a food processor with 1 tablespoon **light olive oil**, 1 large handful **coriander (cilantro) leaves**, 2 tablespoons **lemon juice** and 2 tablespoons **soy sauce** and blend to a smooth paste. Place in a shallow dish with 4 **swordfish steaks**, rubbing the paste evenly all over the fish. Cover and set aside for 10 minutes, or refrigerate for a few hours. Heat a grill plate or barbecue to very hot and cook for 2–3 minutes each side. Serve with a simple **green salad, pilaff, couscous** or **vegetable curry**.

zesty lime pickle rice

Heat a splash of **vegetable oil** in a saucepan and stir-fry 1 chopped **onion** for 2–3 minutes, until softened. Add 3 tablespoons finely chopped **lime pickle** and a good grinding of **black pepper** to the pan and cook for a couple of minutes to bring out the hidden aromatics in the pickle. Add 200 g (7 oz/1 cup) **long-grain rice** (try basmati or jasmine) and stir around for 2 minutes to coat all the grains in the seasonings. Pour in 500 ml (17 fl oz/2 cups) water or **chicken stock** (for more flavour), stir once and bring to the boil. Reduce the heat to low and cover the pan with a tight-fitting lid. Cook for 20 minutes then remove the pan from the heat and leave the lid on for a further 5 minutes. Stir through 2 tablespoons **lime juice** and a handful of chopped **coriander (cilantro) leaves**, fluffing up with a fork.

pumpkin with lime pickle dressing

Combine 2 tablespoons finely chopped **lime pickle**, 1 tablespoon **tamari** or **light soy sauce**, a pinch of **sugar** and 1 tablespoon water until smooth. Cook 450 g (1 lb/ 3 cups) peeled and cubed **pumpkin (winter squash)** in boiling water for 10 minutes, until cooked through but still firm. Drain well and toss the warm pumpkin in a bowl with the lime pickle sauce, 1 large handful **coriander (cilantro) leaves**, chopped, and some **black pepper**.

long-grain rice is also used in recipes on pages...

121, 137, 145 and 203.

long-grain rice

three ways with

prawn, leek and pine nut fried rice

Beat 2 **eggs** in a large bowl and add 555–740 g (1 lb 4 oz–1 lb 10 oz/ 3–4 cups) **cooked long-grain white rice**, stirring around to evenly combine the rice with the egg. Heat 3 tablespoons **vegetable oil** in a hot wok and stir-fry 2 sliced **leeks**, 80 g (2³/4 oz/¹/2 cup) **pine nuts** and 2 crushed **garlic cloves** for a few seconds, so the nuts start to turn golden and the leeks soften. Add 24 peeled and deveined **raw small prawns (shrimp)** and stir-fry for 2 minutes, so the prawns turn pink and curly. Add the rice mixture with 1 teaspoon **sea salt** and stir-fry for 4–5 minutes, constantly tossing the rice to evenly combine the flavours.

ham and egg fried rice

Beat 4 **eggs** in a large bowl and add 555–740 g (1 lb 4 oz–1 lb 10 oz/ 3–4 cups) **cooked long-grain white rice**, stirring around to evenly combine the rice with the egg. Heat 3 tablespoons **light cooking oil** and 1 teaspoon **sesame oil** in a wok or large frying pan and stir-fry 310 g (11 oz/ 2 cups) **sliced ham** for 2–3 minutes, so the ham crisps and flavours the oil nicely. Add 4 finely sliced **spring onions (scallions)** and stir-fry for a few seconds. Add the rice to the wok and stir-fry for 5–6 minutes, so the egg cooks and starts to brown. Stir through 1 tablespoon **light soy sauce** and 155 g (5¹/2 oz/1 cup) **peas** (defrosted if using frozen), cook for 1–2 minutes and serve.

chicken biryani

Have your oven hot and ready at 180°C (350°F/Gas 4). Cook 400 g (14 oz/2 cups) **basmati rice** and 2 teaspoons **turmeric** in boiling water for 5 minutes and drain well. Heat a splash of **olive oil** and 20 g (³/4 oz) **butter** in a casserole dish. When the butter sizzles, add 1 sliced **red onion** and stir-fry for 5 minutes, so the onion starts to darken. Add 2 tablespoons **mild Indian curry paste** and stir-fry for a minute, to bring out the spices in the paste. Add 2 **skinless, boneless chicken breasts**, cut into bite-sized pieces, and stir-fry for 2 minutes. Add the rice to the dish and stir around well to coat the rice in the spicy oil. Add 500 ml (17 fl oz/2 cups) **chicken stock**, bring the mixture to the boil and cover with a tight-fitting lid. Cook in the oven for 40 minutes and serve with **yoghurt** and **lemon wedges**.

long pasta is also used in recipes on pages...
19, 27, 41, 47, 75, 93, 105 and 197.

long pasta

the easiest spaghetti sauce

Cook 400 g (14 oz) **spaghetti** in boiling water for 8–10 minutes. Drain and return to the warm pan. Meanwhile, put 3 tablespoons good **olive oil**, 4 chopped ripe and tasty **tomatoes**, 2 teaspoons rinsed **small capers**, 2 **anchovy fillets** and 1 chopped **garlic clove** in a saucepan and cook over a gentle heat for 3–4 minutes, just to soften everything. Toss the sauce and the spaghetti together and season well. Serve with grated **parmesan**.

smoked chicken linguine

Cook 400 g (14 oz) **linguine** in boiling water for 8–10 minutes. Drain well and return to the warm pan. Meanwhile, stir-fry 1 sliced **red capsicum (pepper)** in a frying pan with a splash of **olive oil** for 2–3 minutes, so the capsicum gently softens but doesn't brown in the oil. Add 250 ml (9 fl oz/ 1 cup) **pouring (whipping) cream** and boil for 5 minutes, so the cream thickens slightly. Add 350 g (12 oz/2 cups) shredded **smoked chicken** (or leftover turkey), 1 tablespoon rinsed **capers** and a handful of roughly chopped **flat-leaf (Italian) parsley**. Add to the pasta with 50 g (1¾ oz/ ½ cup) grated **parmesan** and a good grinding of **black pepper** and stir to evenly coat the pasta in the sauce.

spaghetti with fried sardines, parsley and lemon

Cook 400 g (14 oz) **spaghetti** in boiling water for 8–10 minutes. Drain well and return to the pot. Meanwhile, heat 3 tablespoons good **olive oil** in a frying pan and add 105 g (3¾ oz) tinned **sardines**, drained of oil, and cook for a few minutes over a high heat so the sardines start to brown and crisp. Add 3 chopped **garlic cloves** and 1 chopped **small red chilli** (optional) and cook for a few more minutes so the garlic browns nicely, but doesn't burn. Add a handful of chopped **flat-leaf (Italian) parsley** and 2 tablespoons **lemon juice**. Add the sauce to the pasta, toss and season well. Serve with some grated **parmesan** on the side.

madeira cake

three ways with

sicilian grape and mascarpone cake

Cut a **madeira (pound) cake** in half through the middle. Whip together 3 tablespoons **mascarpone**, 125 ml (4 fl oz/^{1}/$_2$ cup) **pouring (whipping) cream** and 3 tablespoons **icing (confectioners') sugar** in a bowl until smooth. Spread over the cake, top with 180 g (6^1/$_2$ oz/1 cup) **red grapes** and sift over some extra **icing sugar**. Double the mixture to make 2 cakes or save the other half of the cake for a trifle or tiramisu.

tiramisu

Roughly break up a **madeira (pound) cake** to give 3 cups of large chunks and place the pieces in a small ceramic dish. Combine 3 tablespoons **espresso coffee** with 3 tablespoons **Marsala** or **dark rum** and pour over the sponge. Beat 3 **egg yolks** with 110 g (3^3/$_4$ oz/^{1}/$_2$ cup) **mascarpone**, 250 ml (9 fl oz/1 cup) **pouring (whipping) cream** and 3 tablespoons **sugar** until smooth and thick. Beat 3 **egg whites** until you have firm peaks and fold into the cream mixture. Spoon over the cake and sprinkle with 1 tablespoon **unsweetened cocoa powder**. Enjoy straight away or refrigerate until needed.

strawberry and passionfruit trifle

Cover the bottom of a small ceramic dish with 1 cm (^{3}/$_4$ inch) thick slices of **madeira (pound) cake**. Pour over 3 tablespoons **sweet sherry** then pour over 250 ml (9 fl oz/1 cup) **ready-made custard**. Toss 250 g (9 oz) halved **strawberries** and 3 tablespoons **passionfruit pulp** in a bowl and spoon evenly over the custard. Beat 250 ml (9 fl oz/1 cup) **pouring (whipping) cream** with 2 tablespoons **icing (confectioners') sugar** to form soft peaks and spoon over the fruit. Top with a sprinkling of lightly toasted **flaked almonds**.

maple syrup is also used in recipes on pages...
41, 61 and 163.

maple syrup

three ways with

five-spice maple glazed pork

Combine 3 tablespoons **maple syrup**, 1 tablespoon **dark soy sauce** and 1 teaspoon **five-spice** in a dish and add 8 **pork spare ribs**. (about 12 cm/4¹/2 inches long). Toss the pork around to coat in the syrupy mix. Have a grill plate or frying pan hot and ready to go. Add a splash of **light cooking oil** and cook the pork for 4 minutes each side (reduce the heat if the pork begins to burn). Remove from the heat and allow to rest on a plate for a few minutes. Serve on a bed of some blanched **broccolini** (or your favourite greens) and **rice**.

maple custard

Whisk together 125 ml (4 fl oz/ ¹/2 cup) **maple syrup**, 250 ml (9 fl oz/1 cup) **pouring (whipping) cream** and 3 **egg yolks** in a heatproof bowl. Bring a small saucepan of water to a rapid simmer and place the bowl on top. Cook over the simmering water for 8–10 minutes, stirring pretty much all the time, until the custard is silky smooth and thickened. Take the bowl off the water and set aside. If you cover the top of the custard with some plastic wrap at this point, it will prevent a skin forming on top. Enjoy spooned over **grilled peaches** or a **berry fruit salad**.

maple pears

Put 250 ml (9 fl oz/1 cup) **maple syrup**, 250 ml (9 fl oz/1 cup) water, 1 **cinnamon stick** and 2 **cloves** in a saucepan and bring to the boil. Add 4 peeled, cored and quartered **pears** and simmer for 20 minutes. Allow the pears to cool in the mixture and serve with **ice cream** or **mascarpone**, or thinly slice and serve with a cheese platter.

maple syrup / pantry

marmalade

three ways with

orange and chilli ribs

Bring a large pot of water to boil. Add 16 **American-style pork ribs** and cook for 10 minutes. Drain and place in a bowl. Combine 250 ml (9 fl oz/1 cup) **chicken stock**, 3 tablespoons **orange marmalade**, 1 tablespoon **fish sauce** and 1 tablespoon **dark soy sauce** in a bowl. Heat a splash of **light cooking oil** in a really hot wok and stir-fry the pork ribs for 3–4 minutes. Add 1½ teaspoons **chilli flakes** and 1 teaspoon **ground coriander** and stir-fry for a minute. Pour the sauce mixture in and boil for 10–15 minutes, until syrupy and thickly coating the ribs. Serve as a finger-food starter.

star anise and orange duck

Chop a **Chinese barbecued duck** into 10–12 pieces. Boil 250 ml (9 fl oz/1 cup) **rice wine**, 250 ml (9 fl oz/1 cup) **chicken stock**, 160 g (5¾ oz/½ cup) **marmalade**, 2 tablespoons **fish sauce**, 2 **star anise** and 1 **cinnamon stick** in a saucepan for 10 minutes. Add the duck and cook on a rapid simmer for 15 minutes so the sauce really thickens and coats the duck pieces. Serve with **rice** and **steamed Chinese greens**.

ginger and marmalade bread puddings

Have your oven hot and ready at 180°C (350°F/Gas 4). **Butter** 4 slices of **white bread** (crusts removed) then generously spread each slice with **marmalade**. Place the bread to fit snugly in a well-buttered 1 litre (35 fl oz/4 cup) baking dish. Combine 500 ml (17 fl oz/2 cups) **pouring (whipping) cream**, 3 **eggs**, 2 tablespoons **sugar** and 1 teaspoon **ground ginger**, and pour over the bread. Sprinkle **sugar** over the top and bake for 40–45 minutes until puffed and golden. Serve with **custard** or **ice cream**.

meringues are also used in recipes on pages...
61 and 69.

meringues

three ways with

banoffee meringue pie

Break 8 **small meringues** (about 8 cm/3¼ inches across) into bite-sized pieces and place in a ceramic pie dish. Heat 60 g (2¼ oz) **butter**, 140 g (5 oz/¾ cup) **soft brown sugar** and 250 ml (9 fl oz/1 cup) **thick (double/heavy) cream** in a saucepan and stir over a gentle heat until it is totally smooth and looks like caramel velvet. Remove from the heat and allow to cool to room temperature, when it will thicken a little. Thinly slice 4 **bananas** over the meringues and spoon the caramel over the top. Beat 300 ml (10½ fl oz) **pouring (whipping) cream** with 2 tablespoons **icing (confectioners') sugar** until the mixture has thickened to firm peaks. Spoon over the bananas and sprinkle 40 g (1½ oz/¼ cup) chopped **peanuts** on top.

tropical pav

Break 6–8 **small meringues** (about 8 cm/3¼ inches across) into large pieces and place them in a serving dish. Lightly beat 125 ml (4 fl oz/½ cup) **pouring (whipping) cream** with 2 tablespoons **icing (confectioners') sugar** to form soft peaks. Spoon the cream over the meringues. Top with 2 thinly sliced **bananas**, a cubed **mango** and cover the fruit with 3 tablespoons **passionfruit pulp**.

drunken chocolate ice cream meringues

Break a 200 g (7 oz) block of **dark chocolate** into small pieces. Pour 3 tablespoons **thick (double/heavy) cream** in a saucepan and stir over a gentle heat until it is almost about to boil. Add the chocolate, piece by piece, to the hot cream, stirring until all the chocolate is incorporated and the sauce is silky smooth. Remove from the heat and stir in 3 tablespoons **Grand Marnier** or **Frangelico**. Cut the tops off 4 individual **meringues**, spoon a big scoop of **vanilla ice cream** onto each one and generously pour the indulgent sauce over.

miso

three ways with

slow-cooked miso and ginger pork belly

Have your oven hot and ready at 160°C (315°F/Gas 2–3). Heat 1 tablespoon **vegetable oil** in a heavy-based frying pan. Cook a 500–600 g (1 lb 2 oz–1 lb 5 oz) piece of **pork belly**, skin side down, in the smoking hot oil for 2–3 minutes, so the skin is golden. Cook for a minute each on the other sides. Place the pork, skin side down, and 6 slices of **ginger** in a casserole dish. Combine 500 ml (17 fl oz/2 cups) hot water with 4 tablespoons **miso paste** and 2 tablespoons **soft brown sugar**. Stir to dissolve the miso and pour over the pork. Cover with a tight-fitting lid and cook in the oven for 2½ hours, turning after 1 hour. Remove the pork from the hot liquid and allow to cool for 10 minutes. Boil 250 ml (9 fl oz/ 1 cup) of the sauce for 5 minutes, to thicken a little. Slice the pork and serve with **rice** and some of the sauce poured over.

silky leek and miso risotto

Boil 1 litre (35 fl oz/4 cups) water and add 1 teaspoon **dashi granules** and 1 tablespoon **miso paste**. Reduce the heat to a low simmer. Cook 2 finely sliced **leeks** and 1 chopped **garlic clove** in 40 g (1½ oz) of gently sizzling **butter** for 5 minutes, stirring often, so the leeks are silky soft. Add 220 g (7¾ oz/1 cup) **short-grain** or **arborio rice**, stir for a minute then add 125 ml (4 fl oz/½ cup) of the hot stock. Stir until almost all the liquid has been absorbed and repeat the process until all the stock has been used. This may take about 25 minutes. Stir through 50 g (1¾ oz/½ cup) grated **parmesan**, a handful of finely chopped **flat-leaf (Italian) parsley** and an extra 20 g (¾ oz) **butter**. Serve with a little extra parmesan on top.

miso and lemon thyme crumbed lamb fillets

Rub 2 tablepoons **miso paste** evenly over 2 **large lamb backstrap** or **loin fillets**. Combine 100 g (3½ oz/1 cup) **breadcrumbs** (if you can get your hands on them, try using the excellent Japanese breadcrumbs, panko) with 1 teaspoon finely chopped **lemon thyme** and a small handful of **flat-leaf (Italian) parsley**, finely chopped. Roll the lamb in the crumb mix, pressing down firmly to evenly coat the lamb. Heat a couple of splashes of **light olive oil** in a frying pan and cook the fillets in the sizzling hot oil for 3–4 minutes each side (or 1 minute each side if using loin fillets). Remove and allow to rest for a couple of minutes before slicing on an angle and serving with **pumpkin (winter squash) mash** or a **baby English spinach leaf salad**.

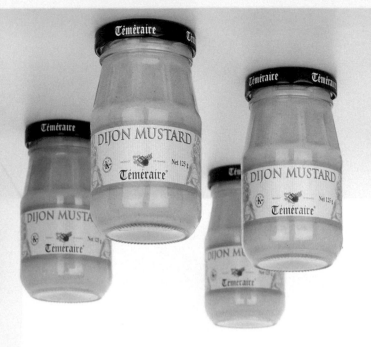

mustard is also used in recipes on pages...
13, 21, 23, 37, 43, 103, 105, 131 and 183.

mustard
three ways with

mustard and herb crumbed veal cutlets

Smear 2 tablepoons of your favourite **mustard** over 4 **veal cutlets**. Combine 80 g (2 3/4 oz/ 1 cup) **breadcrumbs**, 1 teaspoon each **dried oregano** and **dried basil** in a bowl with a good pinch of **salt** and **black pepper**. Press the crumb mixture firmly into each veal cutlet, to cover all over. Heat some **light olive oil** and 40 g (1 1/2 oz) **butter** over a gentle heat, so the butter bubbles. Add the cutlets and cook for 6 minutes each side, until a golden crust is formed. Serve with **pumpkin (winter squash) mash**, **coleslaw** or **green salad**.

tomato, basil and mustard tart

Have your oven hot and ready at 220°C (425°F/Gas 7). Fold over the edges of a sheet of frozen **puff pastry** to make a 1 cm (1/2 inch) border and press down with the back of a fork. Place on a baking tray lined with baking paper and bake for 10 minutes. Remove and spread 1 tablespoon **mild mustard** over the hot tart and lay 2 finely sliced ripe and tasty **tomatoes** on the tart. Season well, drizzle with good **olive oil** and return to the oven for 8–10 minutes, so the tart is really golden and the tomatoes warm and soft. Sprinkle a handful of chopped **kalamata olives** and a handful of torn **basil** over the tart, cut into quarters and enjoy as a starter.

potato salad with mustard basil dressing

Put 125 g (4 1/2 oz/1/2 cup) good **mayonnaise** in a food processor with 2 tablespoons **mild mustard**, 2 chopped **garlic cloves** and 1 handful **basil** and process until the basil is chopped finely in the mixture. Put 12 **baby potatoes** (try nicola) in a saucepan and cover with cold water. Place on a high heat. As soon as the water boils, remove from the heat and place on a tight-fitting lid for 20 minutes. Drain and toss the warm potatoes in the dressing. Season well and serve at a barbecue.

oats

three ways with

creamy oat and raspberry pudding

Place 100 g (3¹/₂ oz/1 cup) **rolled (porridge) oats** in a frying pan and cook over a gentle heat, shaking the pan constantly for a few minutes so they warm through evenly. Put in a bowl and allow to cool. Add 125 ml (4 fl oz/ ¹/₂ cup) **thickened (whipping) cream**, 1 tablespoon **honey** and 2 tablespoons **icing (confectioners') sugar** to the oats and stir to evenly combine. Fold through 150 g (5¹/₂ oz/1 cup) defrosted frozen **raspberries**. Serve with some extra **honey** drizzled over.

coconut, maple and pecan granola

Place 200 g (7 oz/2 cups) **rolled (porridge) oats**, 45 g (1¹/₂ oz/ ¹/₂ cup) **desiccated coconut** and 125 g (4¹/₂ oz/1 cup) chopped **pecans** in a baking tray and cook in a hot oven for 10 minutes, occasionally stirring the oats from the edge into the centre so they cook and golden evenly. Stir 3 tablespoons **maple syrup** through the hot mixture and return to the oven for just a few minutes. Stir well so the sweet maple syrup coats the ingredients. Store in a container and enjoy with **yoghurt** or **milk,** or stir through **dried blueberries**.

apple crumble

Have your oven hot and ready at 220°C (425°F/Gas 7). Peel and slice 3 **apples** directly into a saucepan with 20 g (³/₄ oz) **butter**, 1 tablespoon **sugar** and 1 teaspoon **natural vanilla extract** and cook for 5–6 minutes, to soften the apples. Place the apples in an ovenproof dish. Put 50 g (1³/₄ oz/¹/₂ cup) **rolled (porridge) oats**, 60 g (2¹/₄ oz/¹/₂ cup) **plain (all-purpose) flour**, 3 tablespoons **soft brown sugar** and 40 g (1¹/₂ oz) cold **butter** in a food processor and blend until the mixture looks like coarse breadcrumbs. Sprinkle over the fruit and bake for 10 minutes, just until the top goes golden. Enjoy with **vanilla ice cream** or **custard**.

oyster sauce is also used in recipes on pages...
29, 33, 51, 125, 173 and 185.

oyster sauce

three ways with

stir-fried beef with broccolini and oyster sauce

Finely slice 500 g (1 lb 2 oz) rump steak or beef fillet across the grain and toss around in a bowl with 1 tablespoon rice wine (or white wine) and 1 tablespoon light soy sauce. Set aside for 10 minutes. Heat 3 tablespoons vegetable oil in a wok until smoking hot and stir-fry half of the beef for 1 minute. Remove the beef to a plate, reheat the oil and repeat with the remaining beef. Drain all but 1 tablespoon of oil from the wok and stir-fry 4 sliced spring onions (scallions), 2 chopped garlic cloves and 1 teaspoon grated ginger for a few seconds. Add 2 bunches roughly chopped broccolini and stir-fry for 2–3 minutes. Return the beef to the wok with 3 tablespoons each oyster sauce and water, a pinch of sugar and a small splash of sesame oil. Boil for 2 minutes and serve with rice.

san choy bau of pork, mushroom and water chestnut

Soak 4 dried Chinese mushrooms in boiling water for 20 minutes. Cut off the stems and slice the caps, and keep 3 tablespoons of the soaking liquid. Add 2 tablespoons vegetable oil to a really hot wok and stir-fry 2 garlic cloves and 2 teaspoons finely grated ginger for just a few seconds. Add 500 g (1 lb 2 oz) minced (ground) pork and stir-fry for 5 minutes, so it browns evenly. Add the mushroom liquid, 3 tablespoons water, 3 tablespoons oyster sauce and 90 g (3 1/4 oz/ 1/2 cup) chopped water chestnuts to the wok and bring to the boil for a few minutes, so the sauce thickens. Sprinkle over some sliced spring onions (scallions) and serve in fresh butter lettuce leaves.

slow braised gingered beef

Toss 600 g (1 lb 5 oz) chuck or stewing steak, chopped into 3 cm (1 1/4 inch) pieces, in a bowl with 125 ml (4 fl oz/1/2 cup) oyster sauce and 1/2 teaspoon black pepper. Heat 2 tablespoons light cooking oil in a casserole dish over a high heat and cook the beef in batches for 4–5 minutes, turning often so the meat is nicely browned, and set aside. Add 6–8 thick slices of ginger to the pan with 4–6 garlic cloves and 1 sliced onion. Cook for a few minutes to soften the onion then add 750 ml (26 fl oz/3 cups) chicken stock and bring to the boil. Return the meat to the pan, cover and simmer over a low heat for 1 hour. Remove the lid and bring to a rapid boil for 10 minutes, to thicken the sauce, and serve with rice.

panettone

three ways with

plum bruschetta

Halve 8 **plums** and remove the stones. Toss the plums in 2 tablespoons **soft brown sugar**. Cook the plums in 20 g (³/₄ oz) of gently sizzling **butter** and add 2 tablespoons **orange juice** to the pan, shaking the pan so the plums soften. Remove from the heat. Toast 4 thick slices of **panettone** until lightly golden and spread each piece generously with **fresh ricotta**. Spoon the plums and any juices over the top and dust with **icing (confectioners') sugar**.

italian bread and butter pudding

Have your oven hot and ready at 180°C (350°F/Gas 4). Grease a 1–1.5 litre (35–52 fl oz/4–6 cup) baking dish. Cut 4–6 slices of **panettone**, then tear each slice into 2–3 smaller pieces. Spread **butter** on both sides of the bread and lay the pieces in the dish. Beat 4 **eggs**, 3 tablespoons **caster (superfine) sugar**, 500 ml (17 fl oz/ 2 cups) **milk** and 125 ml (4 fl oz/ ¹/₂ cup) **pouring (whipping) cream** in a bowl and pour over the bread. Allow to sit for 10 minutes then bake in the oven for 45–50 minutes, until puffed and golden. Serve warm with **ice cream**.

panettone french toast

Beat 4 **eggs**, 125 ml (4 fl oz/ ¹/₂ cup) **pouring (whipping) cream** and 125 ml (4 fl oz/¹/₂ cup) **milk** in a bowl. Cut 4 thick wedges from a **panettone** then cut each wedge in half. Heat 20 g (³/₄ oz) **butter** in a non-stick frying pan so it gently sizzles, being careful not to burn the butter. Dip 2 slices of panettone in the egg mix, turning over several times so the slices become soggy. Cook for 2 minutes each side, so the egg sets around the edge and the toast is dark golden. Add more butter to the pan and repeat with the remaining bread. Serve with **fresh berries**.

peanuts are also used in recipes on pages...
115, 129 and 157.

peanuts

three ways with

dry, spicy peanut chicken curry

Blend 80 g (2 3/4 oz/1/2 cup) peanuts in a food processor until finely chopped. Toss 6 quartered chicken thigh fillets, 1 teaspoon finely chopped bottled green peppercorns and 2 tablespoons plain (all-purpose) flour around in a bowl, to evenly coat the chicken. Heat 3 tablespoons peanut oil in a frying pan and stir-fry the chicken pieces for 3–4 minutes, to just brown. Remove the chicken, leaving a tablespoon of oil in the pan. Stir-fry 2 tablespoons red curry paste in the pan for 1 minute, to release all the hidden spices in the paste. Add 1 tablespoon soft brown sugar, 250 ml (9 fl oz/1 cup) coconut milk, 2 tablespoons fish sauce and the peanuts. Boil for 8–10 minutes, until really thick. Return the chicken to the pan with 1 small handful Thai basil and cook for 2–3 minutes on a gentle heat, stirring to coat the chicken in the thick spicy sauce.

gunpowder chicken

Heat 3 tablespoons vegetable oil in a hot wok. Add 4 quartered chicken thigh fillets and cook for 2–3 minutes each side, so the chicken is golden and crispy. Remove the chicken and drain all but 1 tablespoon of oil from the wok. Stir-fry 1 chopped garlic clove, 1 teaspoon chilli flakes, 4 spring onions (scallions), chopped into 3 cm (1 1/4 inch) lengths, and 2 teaspoons grated ginger and stir-fry for a few seconds. Add 1 sliced red capsicum (pepper) and 80 g (2 3/4 oz/1/2 cup) unsalted peanuts. Stir-fry for a minute and return the chicken to the wok with 3 tablespoons hoisin sauce, 125 ml (4 fl oz/1/2 cup) chicken stock and 1/2 teaspoon sugar. Bring to a rapid boil for a few minutes, until the sauce is thick and coats all the ingredients. Serve with rice.

thai peanut pesto

Blend 80 g (2 3/4 oz/1/2 cup) peanuts, 1 handful mint, 1 handful basil (preferably Thai basil), 1 handful coriander (cilantro) leaves, 1 seeded small red chilli, 2 tablespoons lime juice, 2 tablespoons fish sauce and 1 tablespoon shaved palm sugar or soft brown sugar in a food processor until smooth. Serve dolloped on sweet potato soup, with roasted pumpkin (winter squash) or tossed through Asian noodles and roast chicken.

peanut butter

three ways with

satay sauce

Combine 250 g (9 oz/1 cup) peanut butter, 1 tablespoon soft brown sugar, 250 ml (9 fl oz/ 1 cup) coconut milk, 1 chopped small red chilli (remove the seeds for a less spicy satay) and a good squeeze of lemon juice in a small saucepan. Bring the mixture to a gentle simmer for 5 minutes, stirring often so the sauce is smooth and thick. Serve over steamed green beans, bean sprouts and sliced hard-boiled eggs for a Javanese-style vegetable salad.

spicy peanut beef with fragrant thai basil

Boil half the coconut milk from a 400 ml (14 fl oz) tin in a frying pan for 5 minutes, stirring often. Add 2–3 tablespoons red curry paste and stir-fry for 2–3 minutes. Add 2 tablespoons peanut butter, 1 tablespoon fish sauce and 1 tablespoon soft brown sugar and cook for 2–3 minutes, stirring constantly to combine. Add the remaining tinned coconut milk. When the mixture boils, add 600 g (1 lb 5 oz) rump steak, sliced into thin strips, cover and cook over a gentle simmer for 5 minutes. Stir through 1 large handful Thai basil and serve with jasmine rice. Top with extra Thai basil and a finely sliced large red chilli.

stir-fried vegetables with peanut noodles

Cover 200 g (7 oz) rice stick noodles with boiling water for 8 minutes then drain well. Combine 3 tablespoons crunchy peanut butter, 2 tablespoons tamarind purée and 1 tablespoon soft brown sugar with 185 ml (6 fl oz/3/4 cup) hot water. Heat a generous splash of vegetable oil in a wok or frying pan and stir-fry 2 chopped garlic cloves and 2 teaspoons grated ginger for just a few seconds to flavour the oil. Add 120 g (41/4 oz/2 cups) broccoli florets and 1 sliced small red capsicum (pepper) and stir–fry for 2–3 minutes. Add 2 handfuls bean sprouts and stir-fry for 2 minutes, so the sprouts wilt. Add the noodles and sauce mixture to the pan and stir-fry for 4–5 minutes, so the noodles and vegetables are evenly coated in the sauce.

pine nuts are also used in recipes on pages...
39, 47, 91, 147 and 183.

pine nuts

three ways with

shell pasta with chilli, pine nuts and broccolini

Cook 400 g (14 oz) **small shell pasta** in boiling water for 8–10 minutes. In the last 2 minutes of cooking add 1 bunch **broccolini**, cut into 3 cm (1¼ inch) lengths, to the water. Drain well and return to the saucepan. Meanwhile, heat a splash of **olive oil** and 60 g (2¼ oz) **butter** in a frying pan over a medium heat. When the butter sizzles, add 4 tablespoons **pine nuts** and 1 teaspoon **chilli flakes**, shaking the pan to evenly brown the pine nuts. Pour over the pasta, add 50 g (1¾ oz/½ cup) finely grated **parmesan** or **ricotta**, season well and toss to evenly combine. Serve with some extra **parmesan** on top, or toss through some **ricotta** to taste.

persian lamb pizza

Have your oven hot and ready at 220°C (425°F/Gas 7). Heat a splash of **olive oil** in a frying pan and cook 1 sliced **onion** and 2 chopped **garlic cloves** for 4–5 minutes in the sizzling oil, until golden. Add 1 teaspoon each **ground cumin**, **ground coriander** and **sea salt**, and cook for 1 minute. Add 300 g (10½ oz) **minced (ground) lamb** and stir-fry for 5 minutes, until evenly browned. Spread the lamb mixture over a round piece of **pitta bread**, top with 3 tablespoons **pine nuts** and cook in the oven for 5–8 minutes, so the bread crisps up and the nuts are golden. Enjoy with a **green salad** and some **hummus** on the side. Serves 2.

spicy chicken and pine nut san choy bau

Heat a splash of **vegetable oil** in a wok or frying pan and stir-fry 3 tablespoons **pine nuts**, 2 chopped **garlic cloves** and 1 seeded and chopped **small red chilli** for a few seconds until aromatic and the pine nuts start to turn golden. Add 500 g (1 lb 2 oz) **minced (ground) chicken** and stir-fry for 5 minutes, so the chicken browns evenly. Add 2 tablespoons **oyster sauce**, 1 tablespoon **light soy sauce** and a good pinch of **sugar** to the pan and stir-fry for a few more minutes. Have some crisp **iceberg lettuce leaves** washed and rinsed to roll up the tasty stir-fry.

polenta is also used in a recipe on page...
65.

polenta

three ways with

baked polenta pie

Have your oven hot and ready at 180°C (350°F/Gas 4). Lightly grease a round ovenproof dish, no larger than 20 cm (8 inches) across, and sprinkle with 1 tablespoon **instant polenta**. Combine 75 g (2½ oz/½ cup) **instant polenta**, 250 ml (9 fl oz/1 cup) water, 3 tablespoons **self-raising flour**, 50 g (1¾ oz/½ cup) grated **parmesan**, 1 handful **flat-leaf (Italian) parsley**, chopped, and a good squeeze of **lemon juice** in a bowl, stirring to combine really well and spoon into the dish. Bake for 30 minutes. Allow to cool a little before turning out and cutting into wedges to serve as a substitute for mashed potato. Leftover pie can also be sliced and pan-fried in hot oil until golden.

herbed chicken schnitzel

Cut 2 **skinless, boneless chicken breasts** through the middle to give 4 thinner pieces. Put the chicken between 2 layers of plastic wrap and gently beat until 5 mm (¼ inch) thick. Put 125 g (4½ oz/ 1 cup) **well-seasoned flour** in a bowl, 4 beaten **eggs** in another bowl and in a third bowl combine 150 g (5½ oz/1 cup) **instant polenta**, 50 g (1¾ oz/½ cup) grated **parmesan** and 2 teaspoons **dried oregano**. Dip the chicken in the flour, then in the beaten egg and, finally, press the chicken firmly into the herbed polenta mixture to evenly coat. Heat 250 ml (9 fl oz/ 1 cup) **vegetable oil** in a frying pan and cook the schnitzels in the hot, sizzling oil for 3–4 minutes each side. Serve with creamy **mash**.

tomato gratin

Have your oven hot and ready at 180°C (350°F/Gas 4). Cut 4 ripe and tasty **tomatoes** in half. Combine 3 tablespoons **instant polenta**, 1 teaspoon **thyme leaves** (or ½ teaspoon dried oregano) and a good seasoning of **salt** and **black pepper** in a bowl and press the cut side of the tomatoes firmly into the polenta mixture. Heat a splash of **olive oil** and 20 g (¾ oz) **butter** in a non-stick frying pan and cook the tomatoes, cut side down, for 3–4 minutes so they form a golden crust. Transfer to a baking tray, pour over any pan juices, sprinkle with 3 tablespoons grated **parmesan** and bake in the oven for 30 minutes, until the tomatoes are really soft and juicy.

red and brown lentils are also used in a recipe on page...
119.

red and brown lentils

three ways with

lentil and bean curry

Cook 250 g (9 oz/1 cup) **red** or **brown lentils** in boiling water for 30 minutes and drain. Cook 1 chopped **onion** and 2 chopped **garlic cloves** in 40 g (1¹/₂ oz) of sizzling **butter** for 2–3 minutes. Add 1 tablespoon **curry powder** and cook for 1 minute, to bring out the hidden spices in the powder. Add 400 g (14 oz) tinned **chopped tomatoes**, 500 ml (17 fl oz/2 cups) water and 3 handfuls trimmed and halved **green beans**, and boil. Cook on a rapid simmer for 10 minutes. Add the lentils and cook for a further 10 minutes, until thick and the lentils are really soft.

mediterranean lentil soup

Stir-fry 1 chopped **onion** and 1 chopped **garlic clove** in 60 g (2¹/₄ oz) sizzling **butter** for a few minutes, to soften the onion. Add 250 g (9 oz/1 cup) **red** or **brown lentils**, 400 g (14 oz) tinned **chopped tomatoes**, 2 tablespoons **sun-dried tomato paste (concentrated purée)** and 750 ml (26 fl oz/3 cups) **chicken stock** to the pan and bring to the boil. Reduce the heat and simmer for 45 minutes, stirring often, until the lentils are soft and creamy. Serve with buttered fingers of toasted **Turkish (pide/flat) bread**.

chicken with spiced buttered lentils

Cook 125 g (4¹/₂ oz/¹/₂ cup) **red** or **brown lentils** in boiling water for 30 minutes and drain well. Put 1 chopped **onion**, 1 **garlic clove**, a 2 cm (³/₄ inch) piece of **ginger** and 1 tablespoon **vegetable oil** in a food processor and blend to a smooth paste. Stir-fry 4 quartered **chicken thigh fillets** in a splash of hot **vegetable oil** for 5 minutes, until nicely browned. Add the onion mixture, 2 tablespoons **mild curry powder** and stir-fry for 5 minutes, to release all the hidden spices in the powder. Add the lentils, 1 chopped **carrot** and 500 ml (17 fl oz/2 cups) water to the pan and simmer for 15 minutes, until thickened. Stir through 40 g (1¹/₂ oz) **butter** and a handful of chopped **coriander (cilantro) leaves** and cook on a gentle heat for 5 minutes. Serve with **basmati rice** and warm **naan bread**.

red and brown lentils / pantry

red curry paste is also used in recipes on pages...
75, 169 and 171.

red curry paste

spicy red chicken

Have your oven hot and ready at
180°C (350°F/Gas 4). Combine
2 tablespoons **red curry paste** in a
bowl with 40 g (1½ oz) **butter** and
6–8 finely chopped **basil leaves**.
Rub this mixture under the skin of
4 **chicken breasts** (on the bone).
Place the chicken on a baking tray
and into the oven for 30 minutes.
Serve the chicken with stir-fried
green beans and **rice**.

fruity duck curry

Cook 125 ml (4 fl oz/½ cup)
coconut cream in a saucepan over
a high heat for 5–6 minutes, so
little bubbling holes form and it
starts to turn brown around the
edge of the pan. Add 2 tablespoons
red curry paste and stir-fry for
2 minutes. Add 2 tablespoons
shaved **palm sugar** or **soft brown
sugar** and stir-fry for 1 minute.
Add 1 litre (35 fl oz/4 cups)
coconut milk and bring to the boil.
Add 1 **Chinese barbecued duck**,
chopped into 10–12 pieces, to
the pan with 250 g (9 oz) **cherry
tomatoes**, 1 small handful **grapes**,
1 small handful **fresh** or **tinned
lychees**, 80 g (2¾ oz/½ cup)
chopped **pineapple** and a handful
of **Thai basil**. Bring to the boil
then reduce the heat to simmer for
10 minutes, to soften the fruit. Stir
through 2 tablespoons **fish sauce**
and serve with **rice**.

spicy thai lamb cutlets with beans and basil

Heat 3 tablespoons **vegetable oil** in
a large frying pan. Cook 2 handfuls
trimmed and halved **green beans**
and stir-fry for 2 minutes, then set
aside. Cook 12 **lamb cutlets**, in
two batches, in the hot oil for
1 minute each side. Remove the
lamb and drain all but 1 tablespoon
of oil from the pan. Stir-fry
1 tablespoon **red curry paste**
and 2 chopped **garlic cloves** for
1 minute. Add 125 ml (4 fl oz/
½ cup) water, 1 tablespoon **sugar**
and 2 tablespoons **fish sauce** and
stir-fry until the paste is smooth
and well-combined, then boil the
sauce for 2–3 minutes. Return the
beans and lamb to the pan with
a handful of torn **Thai basil** and
4 torn **makrut (kaffir lime) leaves**
and simmer for 5 minutes, turning
the cutlets over in the pan, to
coat in the sauce. Serve with
jasmine rice.

red wine is also used in recipes on pages...

13, 131 and 203.

red wine

three ways with

red wine and beef casserole

Have your oven hot and ready at 180°C (350°F/Gas 4). Cut 600 g (1 lb 5 oz) **chuck** or **stewing steak** into large cubes and put in a bowl with 60 g (2 1/4 oz/1/2 cup) **plain (all-purpose) flour** and **salt** and **black pepper**. Toss the beef cubes around to coat in the flour. Heat a splash of **olive oil** and 20 g (3/4 oz) **butter** in a casserole dish and cook the beef in batches, so the meat sizzles and browns in the pan. Put the browned meat aside. Add 1 chopped **onion** and 2 chopped **bacon slices** to the pan and cook for 5 minutes, so the onion gently sizzles in the pan. Return the meat to the pan with 250 ml (9 fl oz/ 1 cup) **red wine**, 400 g (14 oz) tinned **chopped tomatoes**, 125 ml (4 fl oz/1/2 cup) water, 90 g (3 1/4 oz/1 cup) chopped **button mushrooms** and 1 **bay leaf**. Cook in the oven for 1 1/2 hours and serve with **potato mash**.

slow-cooked octopus in red wine, tomato and olive sauce

Put 2 chopped **small onions** and 2 **garlic cloves** in a food processor with 3 tablespoons good **olive oil** and process to a smooth paste. Put in a heavy-based saucepan with 250 ml (9 fl oz/1 cup) **red wine**, 400 g (14 oz) tinned **chopped tomatoes**, a handful of **small black olives** and a handful of roughly chopped **flat-leaf (Italian) parsley** and bring to the boil. Add 8 cleaned **small octopus** (cut the tentacles in half if too big), reduce the heat to low and simmer for 1 hour.

red wine and vanilla figs

Pour 250 ml (9 fl oz/1 cup) **red wine** into a saucepan. Split a **vanilla bean** and scape out the seeds. Add the seeds and the bean pod to the saucepan along with 110 g (3 3/4 oz/1/2 cup) **sugar**, and boil for 5 minutes. Add 4 **figs**, simmer for 2–3 minutes then place on a lid and turn off the heat. Let the figs sit in the vanilla wine for 10 minutes. Eat the figs warm or at room temperature with **cream** or **ice cream**. Stored in the fridge overnight, the figs will have a more intense flavour.

red wine vinegar is also used in recipes on pages...
17, 63, 65, 103, 111, 123, 131, 207 and 213.

red wine vinegar

three ways with

avocado and crispy prosciutto salad

Combine 1 crushed **garlic clove**, 1 teaspoon **mustard**, 3 tablespoons **olive oil** and 2 tablespoons **red wine vinegar** in a small bowl and whisk to combine. Heat a generous splash of **olive oil** in a non-stick frying pan and cook 6–8 slices of **prosciutto** for 2–3 minutes each side, until crispy. Put the prosciutto and any of the tasty oil from the pan in a large bowl with 2 **avocados**, cut into thick wedges, a handful of **roasted capsicum (peppers)**, torn into strips, and 3 large handfuls **baby rocket (arugula)** or **English spinach leaves**. Pour over the dressing, gently toss to combine the ingredients and serve.

herbed caponata

Cook 1 finely cubed **eggplant (aubergine)** in 3 tablespoons hot **olive oil** until dark golden, stirring often so the eggplant cooks evenly. Add 1 diced **red capsicum (pepper)** and 2 chopped **celery stalks**, and cook for a minute, so the celery stays a little crunchy. Add 2 chopped **anchovy fillets**, 1 tablespoon rinsed **capers**, 110 g (3 3/4 oz/1/2 cup) chopped **green olives**, 2 tablespoons **tomato paste (concentrated purée)**, 3 tablespoons **red wine vinegar** and 2 teaspoons **sugar**, and cook for 5 minutes. Stir through a handful of roughly chopped **mint**. Toss through your favourite pasta, add to **bruschetta** or serve as a side to **grilled lamb**.

sicilian chicken and pine nut pasta salad

Cook 400 g (14 oz) **very small pasta** (try orzo or risoni) in boiling water until *al dente* (different varieties require different cooking times). Drain well and add a little splash of **olive oil** to the pasta, tossing through with your hands so they stay separated, and allow to cool. Cook 1 finely sliced **red capsicum (pepper)** in a splash of **olive oil** in a saucepan for a couple of minutes then add 3 tablespoons **red wine vinegar** and 1 tablespoon **soft brown sugar**. Place on a lid and cook over a low heat for 5 minutes. Add to the pasta 350 g (12 oz/2 cups) shredded **smoked chicken**, 3 tablespoons lightly toasted **pine nuts**, 1 large handful roughly chopped **flat-leaf (Italian) parsley** and 60 g (2 1/4 oz/1/2 cup) **sultanas (golden raisins)**. Toss to combine, season well and serve.

rice wine is also used in recipes on pages...
87, 155 and 165.

rice wine

three ways with

sweet soy chicken wings

Cut the tips off 8 **chicken wings** and discard. Cut between the middle joint to give 16 perfect finger-food pieces. Heat 250 ml (9 fl oz/1 cup) **vegetable oil** in a wok. When the surface of the oil shimmers, carefully add a handful of the chicken and fry for 5 minutes, turning often so the pieces golden evenly. Remove to some paper towel and repeat, reheating the oil between each batch. Discard the oil and return all the chicken to the wok with 125 ml (4 fl oz/1/2 cup) **rice wine**, 125 ml (4 fl oz/1/2 cup) **chicken stock**, 2 chopped **garlic cloves**, a few thick slices of **ginger**, 3 tablespoons **dark soy sauce** and 3 tablespoons **soft brown sugar**. Bring to a rapid boil then reduce the heat to low and cover with a lid for 8–10 minutes. Remove the lid and increase the heat. Gently stir-fry for 2–3 minutes until the liquid becomes a thick, dark, sweet syrup coating the chicken.

black bean pork and broccoli hotpot

Cut 2 **pork fillets** into bite-sized cubes and toss around in a bowl with 4 tablespoons **black bean sauce**. Heat 2 tablespoons **light cooking oil** in a really hot casserole dish. Stir-fry 4 **spring onions (scallions)**, chopped into 3 cm (1¼ inch) lengths, for a few seconds in the hot oil. Add the pork mixture to the wok and vigorously stir-fry for 4–5 minutes, to evenly brown the pork. Dissolve 2 teaspoons **cornflour (cornstarch)** in 125 ml (4 fl oz/1/2 cup) **rice wine** and pour into the pan with 125 ml (4 fl oz/1/2 cup) **chicken stock**, 1 tablespoon **oyster sauce** and a good pinch of **sugar**. Bring to the boil then add 120 g (4¼ oz/2 cups) **broccoli florets**. Cover with a lid and cook over a low heat for 5 minutes. Serve over **rice**.

drunken chicken

Put 2 **skinless, boneless large chicken breasts** in a saucepan with 500 ml (17 fl oz/2 cups) **rice wine**, 1 tablespoon **salt** and a few thick slices of **ginger**. Add enough water so the chicken is covered and put on a medium heat. As soon as the stock boils, cover the pan with a tight-fitting lid, turn off the heat and set aside for 20 minutes. Remove the chicken and rest for 5 minutes. Thinly slice the chicken, top with a handful of roughly chopped **coriander (cilantro) leaves** and serve with steamed Asian greens, **rice** and **soy sauce** on the side.

salmon is also used in a recipe on page...
67.

salmon

three ways with

salmon shepherd's pie

Have your oven hot and ready at 180°C (350°F/Gas 4). Cook 1 chopped **onion**, 1 tablespoon rinsed **small capers** and 2 tablespoons finely chopped **flat-leaf (Italian) parsley** in 60 g (2¼ oz) hot sizzling **butter** for a few minutes until softened. Add 2 tablespoons **plain (all-purpose) flour** and stir for a minute over a gentle heat until a thick paste is formed. Slowly add 500 ml (17 fl oz/2 cups) **milk**, stirring constantly for a smooth, thick sauce. Stir through 500 g (1 lb 2 oz) tinned **salmon**, drained well and left in chunky pieces. Spoon into a baking dish. Cook 4 chopped **all-purpose large potatoes** in boiling water for 20 minutes. Drain and return to the pan with 40 g (1½ oz) **butter** and 3 tablespoons **milk** and mash until smooth. Spoon over the salmon and bake for 30 minutes.

salmon, potato and dill cakes

Cook 3 chopped **all-purpose potatoes** in boiling water for 10 minutes. Drain and roughly mash, leaving it a bit lumpy. Add 225 g (8 oz) tinned **salmon**, drained well, 2 tablespoons chopped **dill**, 1 chopped **small onion** and 1 **egg** and season well with **salt** and **black pepper**. Divide the mixture into 8, then roll and flatten each into a disc. Dip into a bowl of **plain (all-purpose) flour**, then dip into a bowl of lightly beaten **egg** and finally dip into a bowl of **breadcrumbs**, pressing firmly to evenly coat in the crumbs. Cook the salmon cakes in 125 ml (4 fl oz/½ cup) hot **vegetable oil** for 3–4 minutes each side, so they sizzle. Serve with a **herb and caper mayonnaise**.

salmon omelette

Have your grill (broiler) hot and ready. Beat 3 **eggs** and a splash of water in a bowl. Roughly mash 85 g (3 oz) tinned **salmon**, drained well, and add to the egg with a squeeze of **lemon juice**, 1 handful **flat-leaf (Italian) parsley**, chopped, and 3 tablespoons grated **cheddar**. Heat a little **butter** in a non-stick frying pan. Swirl the pan around to coat in the sizzling butter. Pour in the mixture and cook over a medium heat for 4–5 minutes, so the edges puff up and the bottom turns golden. Place under the grill until puffed up and golden on top. Grind over some **black pepper** and serve with **toast**. Serves 1.

sesame seeds are also used in recipes on pages...
29, 97, 135, 201 and 209.

sesame seeds

three ways with

korean sesame barbecue marinade

Combine 1 tablespoon **sesame seeds** in a ceramic dish with 3 tablespoons **barbecue sauce**, 1 tablespoon **balsamic vinegar**, 2 finely chopped **spring onions (scallions)**, 1 teaspoon grated **ginger**, 1 crushed **garlic clove** and 1/4 teaspoon **chilli powder**. Add your meat and toss around to evenly coat in the marinade. Refrigerate for a few hours or overnight. Remove from the fridge 30 minutes before cooking to your liking on a hot grill or barbecue.

sesame-crusted tuna steaks with wasabi mayonnaise

Put 80 g (2 3/4 oz/1/2 cup) **sesame seeds** on a plate. Press 4 **tuna steaks**, about 180–200 g (6 1/2– 7 oz) each, firmly onto the seeds so they evenly coat the fish. Heat a few splashes of **light olive oil** in a hot non-stick frying pan and cook the tuna for 2–3 minutes each side, so they sizzle in the pan and turn the seeds a dark golden colour. Remove from the pan. Combine 125 g (4 1/2 oz/1/2 cup) **mayonnaise** with 2 teaspoons **wasabi paste**, 1 crushed **garlic clove** and 1 teaspoon **tamari** or **soy sauce**. Serve the mayonnaise with the tuna and **potato mash** or **salad** on the side.

spicy sesame chicken salad

Put 2 teaspoons each **sesame seeds** and **sichuan peppercorns** in a hot, dry frying pan and shake the pan over the heat until the sesame seeds turn an even golden and the peppercorns start to smoke. Remove and allow to cool. Put the mixture in a food processor (or use a mortar and pestle) with 1 teaspoon **chilli flakes**, 2 tablespoons **light soy sauce**, 2 teaspoons **sesame oil** and 1 teaspoon **caster (superfine) sugar** and blend to a paste. Shred the skin and meat of a **barbecued chicken** and toss around in a bowl with 1 sliced **Lebanese (short) cucumber** and 4 finely sliced **spring onions (scallions)**. Add the paste and toss well to evenly coat the chicken in the spicy dressing.

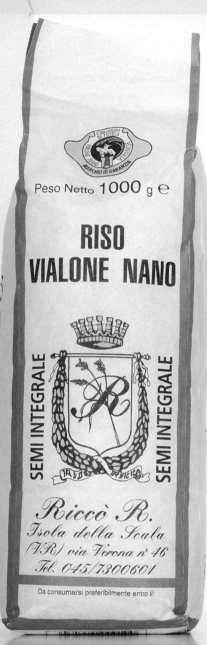

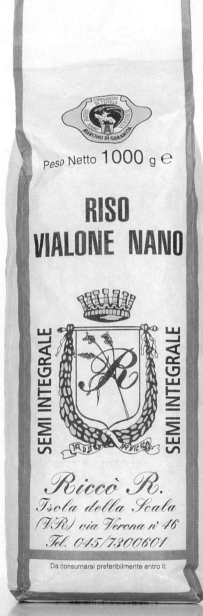

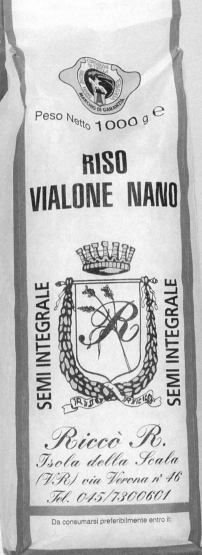

Peso Netto **1000** g ℮

RISO
VIALONE NANO

SEMI INTEGRALE SEMI INTEGRALE

Riccò R.
Isola della Scala
(V.R) via Verona n° 46
Tel. 045/7300601

Da consumarsi preferibilmente entro il:

short-grain rice is also used in recipes on pages...
21, 55 and 159.

short-grain rice

three ways with

baked tuna and zucchini risotto

Have your oven hot and ready at 200°C (400°F/Gas 6). Heat a splash of **olive oil** in a casserole dish and stir-fry 1 chopped **onion** and 2 grated **zucchini (courgettes)** for 2–3 minutes, so the onion softens and sizzles in the hot oil. Add 220 g (7³/₄ oz/1 cup) **short-grain rice** to the pan, stir for a minute then add 225 g (8 oz) tinned **tuna**, drained, 400 g (14 oz) tinned **chopped tomatoes**, 1 teaspoon **rosemary leaves**, 375 ml (13 fl oz/1¹/₂ cups) **chicken stock** and season well with **sea salt** and **black pepper**. Bring to the boil, cover the dish with a tight-fitting lid and cook in the oven for 30 minutes. Scatter a handful of chopped **flat-leaf (Italian) parsley** on top. Serves 2.

niçoise rice salad

Cook 220 g (7³/₄ oz/1 cup) **short-grain rice** in boiling water for 12–15 minutes, so the grains are still slightly firm in the centre. Rinse, drain well and put in a bowl with 225 g (8 oz) tinned **tuna** (add the tasty oil from the tin), 2 finely chopped **anchovy fillets**, 2 chopped firm **tomatoes**, 2 quartered **hard-boiled eggs**, 1 small handful **flat-leaf (Italian) parsley**, finely chopped, 2 tablespoons finely chopped **chives** and 3 tablespoons **black olives**. Gently toss to combine, being careful not to break up the eggs too much. Season well with **salt** and **black pepper** and serve with **lemon wedges** on the side. Serves 2.

baked vanilla rice pudding

Have your oven hot and ready at 160°C (315°F/Gas 2–3). Rub a little **butter** to grease the inside of a 1 litre (35 fl oz/4 cup) baking dish. Combine 750 ml (26 fl oz/3 cups) **milk**, 3 tablespoons **sugar**, 3 eggs and 1 teaspoon **natural vanilla extract** in a bowl. Beat until the eggs are just combined then pour into the prepared dish. Sprinkle 3 tablespoons **short-grain rice** into the custard mixture, sprinkle with a little **ground nutmeg** and bake for 50 minutes. Serve with **cherry** or **fig jam** and **cream**. Serves 4–6.

short pasta is also used in recipes on pages...
13, 19, 23, 37, 49, 71, 81, 91, 173, 183 and 207.

short pasta

three ways with

springtime minestrone

Cook 90 g (3¼ oz/1 cup) **small shell pasta** in boiling water for 8–10 minutes. Heat a splash of **olive oil** in a saucepan and cook 1 chopped **onion** and 1 **thyme sprig** for 5 minutes, so the onion sizzles and softens. Add 1 chopped **garlic clove**, 1 chopped **small carrot**, 2 chopped **celery stalks** and 2 chopped **zucchini (courgettes)** and cook for 3–4 minutes. Add 1.5 litres (52 fl oz/6 cups) **chicken stock** and bring to the boil for 15 minutes. Add the pasta to the soup, season well and stir through a handful of chopped **flat-leaf (Italian) parsley**. Simmer for 5 minutes. Serve topped with some finely grated **parmesan**.

penne with italian sausage, basil and pecorino

Remove the skin from 4 **Italian sausages** and roughly chop the meat. Cook 400 g (14 oz) **penne** for 8–10 minutes in boiling water. Drain and return to the pan. Heat a splash of good **olive oil** in a large saucepan and cook 1 chopped **onion** for a few minutes. Add the sausage meat to the pan and stir-fry for 5 minutes, until browned. Add 400 g (14 oz) tinned **chopped tomatoes**, 1 handful torn **basil**, 125 ml (4 fl oz/½ cup) water and a pinch each of **sugar** and **salt**. Boil for 5 minutes then stir through the pasta and 45 g (1½ oz/½ cup) grated **pecorino**.

chilli pumpkin rigatoni

Cook 400 g (14 oz) **rigatoni** in boiling water for 8 minutes then drain well. Heat 3 tablespoons **light olive oil** in a frying pan and add 300 g (10½ oz/2 cups) peeled and cubed **pumpkin (winter squash)** pieces, 1 chopped **large red chilli** and 2 chopped **garlic cloves**. Stir-fry over a high heat for 2 minutes. Reduce the heat to low, cover and cook for 10 minutes. Stir a few times, then cover and cook for another 4–5 minutes. Put the cooked pumpkin mixture and any oil from the pan in a large bowl with the rigatoni, 1 tablespoon **lemon juice**, 50 g (1¾ oz/½ cup) grated **parmesan** and 2 handfuls **mizuna**. Season with **salt** and **black pepper**, toss to combine and serve warm.

soy sauce is also used in recipes on pages...
15, 17, 29, 33, 51, 65, 87, 93, 95, 97, 109, 125, 127, 133, 135, 145, 147, 153, 155, 165, 173, 185, 189, 197, 201 and 211.

soy sauce

three ways with

red braised pork fillet

Combine 1 litre (35 fl oz/4 cups) chicken stock, 125 ml (4 fl oz/ 1/2 cup) light soy sauce, 2 tablespoons dark soy sauce, 1 teaspoon five-spice, 95 g (3 1/4 oz/1/2 cup) soft brown sugar, 2 garlic cloves and 4–6 thick slices of ginger in a saucepan and boil for 5 minutes. Add 2 pork fillets, reduce the heat to low and cover for 20 minutes, turning the pork halfway through the cooking time. Remove, cover the pork with foil and allow to rest for 5 minutes. Slice and serve with rice or noodles, steamed Asian greens and some of the hot braising liquid spooned over the top.

soy-simmered vegetables with tofu

Boil 750 ml (26 fl oz/3 cups) chicken stock, 3 tablespoons light soy sauce and 2 tablespoons mirin (or 2 teaspoons sugar) in a frying pan. Add 450 g (1 lb/3 cups) peeled and cubed pumpkin (winter squash), 1 chopped carrot, 100 g (3 1/2 oz) shiitake mushrooms and 4 spring onions (scallions), cut into 3 cm (1 1/4 inch) lengths, to the pan. Simmer the vegetables for 10 minutes, turning often. Add 300 g (10 1/2 oz) firm tofu, cut into 2 cm (3/4 in) cubes, and cook for a further 5 minutes. Serve with rice.

ginger teriyaki chicken

Toss 4–6 chicken thigh fillets around in a bowl with 125 ml (4 fl oz/1/2 cup) chicken stock, 3 tablespoons light soy sauce, 2 teaspoons finely grated ginger and a heaped teaspoon of sugar. Marinate for a few hours if you have the time, otherwise heat a grill (barbecue) plate to smoking hot. Shake the excess marinade off the chicken and cook for 5 minutes each side. Quickly boil the marinade for a few minutes, slice the chicken and serve on rice with the hot sauce over and sprinkled with some chilli powder.

stale bread is also used in a recipe on page...
105.

stale bread

three ways with

pasta with chilli crumbs

Cook 400 g (14 oz) **spaghetti** in boiling water for 8–10 minutes. Meanwhile, heat a few splashes of **olive oil** in a frying pan and cook 100 g (3 1/2 oz/1 cup) **breadcrumbs** (stale sourdough makes delicious crumbs) for a few minutes until they start to turn crispy golden. Put in a bowl. Add a few more splashes of **oil** to the pan and cook 3 chopped **garlic cloves**, 1 teaspoon **chilli flakes** and 4–6 chopped **anchovy fillets** and stir-fry for 2 minutes, to flavour the oil. Add the cooked pasta to the pan with the crumbs, 50 g (1 3/4 oz/1/2 cup) grated **parmesan**, a handful of **flat-leaf (Italian) parsley**, roughly chopped, and a good grinding of **black pepper**. Toss around well to combine the ingredients and serve.

crumbed prawns with plum sauce

Place a peeled and deveined **raw large prawn (shrimp)** between 2 layers of plastic wrap and gently pound to flatten. Repeat to make 12 prawn cutlets. Put 2 tablespoons **cornflour (cornstarch)**, 2 beaten **eggs** and 100 g (3 1/2 oz/1 cup) **breadcrumbs** (made with stale bread) in three separate bowls. Toss each prawn in the cornflour, dip into the egg then gently press into the crumbs. Fill a wok one-third full with **vegetable oil** over a medium heat. When the surface of the oil is shimmering, cook the prawns in 2 batches for 2–3 minutes, so the breadcrumbs turn dark golden. Serve with **plum sauce** or 2 tablespoons **light soy sauce** mixed with 1 tablespoon **lemon juice**.

parmesan and herb crumbed lamb cutlets

Whiz-up some **stale bread** in a food processor to make about 200 g (7 oz/2 cups) **breadcrumbs**. Put the crumbs in a bowl, 3 beaten **eggs** in another bowl, and 100 g (3 1/2 oz/1 cup) grated **parmesan** mixed with 1 teaspoon **dried oregano** in a third. Working one at a time, dip a trimmed **lamb cutlet** in the flour, then in the egg then in the herbed parmesan, pressing firmly onto the lamb to coat in the parmesan. Repeat to make 12 cutlets. Heat a few splashes of **light olive oil** in a non-stick frying pan and cook the lamb in batches, over a medium heat, for 3–4 minutes each side, until they look deliciously golden and crispy. Serve with **potato mash** and **beans**.

sweet chilli sauce

three ways with

sticky chilli lime ribs

Cook 16 **American-style pork ribs** in boiling water for 10 minutes. Drain and allow to cool. Combine 250 ml (9 fl oz/1 cup) **chicken stock**, 3 tablespoons **sweet chilli sauce**, 2 tablespoons **lime juice**, 1 teaspoon grated **lime zest** and 2 tablespoons **fish sauce** in a bowl. Heat a splash of **cooking oil** in a really hot wok. Add the ribs and stir-fry for 3–4 minutes. Add the sauce and boil for 8–10 minutes, until the sticky sauce thickly coats the ribs.

barbecued duck rice salad

Heat 2 tablespoons **vegetable oil** in a saucepan. When the oil is just about smoking hot, add 400 g (14 oz/2 cups) **jasmine rice** and stir for 2 minutes, so the rice turns lightly golden and smells nutty. Add 750 ml (26 fl oz/3 cups) **chicken stock** (it will splutter in the pan). As soon as the stock boils, place on a tight-fitting lid and cook on a really low heat for 25 minutes. Remove from the heat, stir a few times and put in a large bowl and allow to cool. Add 1 shredded **Chinese barbecued duck** (or a **barbecued chicken**) to the rice with 125 ml (4 fl oz/ 1/2 cup) **sweet chilli sauce**, 1 finely sliced **small red onion**, 1 finely sliced **Lebanese (short) cucumber** and 1 large handful each roughly chopped **coriander (cilantro) leaves** and **mint**. Toss together well and serve.

chargrilled chilli prawns

Put 125 ml (4 fl oz/1/2 cup) **sweet chilli sauce** in a bowl with 1 teaspoon **ground cumin**, 2 tablespoons finely chopped **coriander (cilantro) leaves and stems** and 1/2 teaspoon **white pepper**. Add 16 peeled and deveined **raw large prawns (shrimp)**, tossing around to coat in the marinade. Cover and refrigerate for 30 minutes, or a few hours if you have the time. Heat a little oil on a smoking-hot chargrill or barbecue hotplate and cook the prawns for 3 minutes each side. Remove and squeeze over some **lime juice** and season with **sea salt**. Serve with **salad**, **wedges** or **mash**.

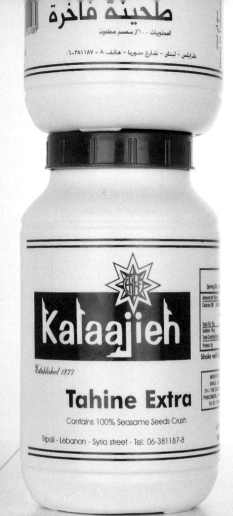

tahini is also used in a recipe on page...

57.

tahini

three ways with

roast pumpkin, tahini and couscous salad

Have your oven hot and ready at 180°C (350°F/Gas 4). Toss 300 g (10½ oz/2 cups) peeled and cubed **pumpkin (winter squash)** in a bowl with a splash of **olive oil**, 1 teaspoon each **ground cumin** and **sea salt**, and a good grinding of **black pepper**. You can also add a pinch of **chilli flakes** or some chopped **fresh chilli** if you like. Place the pumpkin pieces on a baking tray and roast for 30 minutes. Meanwhile, combine 135 g (4¾ oz/½ cup) **tahini**, 2 tablespoons **lemon juice**, 2 crushed **garlic cloves** and 1 teaspoon **sea salt** and stir until smooth. Toss the cooked pumpkin with 2–3 handfuls **baby rocket (arugula) leaves** and spoon over the dressing. Serve with **steamed couscous**.

fried cauliflower with lemon tahini

Whiz-up 3 tablespoons **tahini** in a food processor with 250 g (9 oz/ 1 cup) **Greek-style yoghurt**, 1 teaspoon **ground cumin**, 1 crushed **garlic clove** and 2 tablespoons **lemon juice** until you have a smooth sauce. Season well with **sea salt**. Heat 500 ml (17 fl oz/2 cups) **vegetable oil** in a frying pan so the surface of the oil is gently shimmering. Break large florets off a small head of **cauliflower** and cook several pieces at a time in the oil, turning often until they are golden brown all over. Repeat with the remaining cauliflower florets and serve with the sauce.

bang bang chicken salad

Combine 2 tablespoons **tahini** in a bowl with 1 teaspoon **sesame oil**, 2 tablespoons **light soy sauce** and 1 tablespoon **balsamic** or **Chinese black vinegar**. Toss the shredded meat and skin of a **barbecued chicken** in a bowl with 2 sliced **cucumbers** and 3 sliced **spring onions (scallions)**. Pour over the sauce, gently toss and serve the salad on several leaves of **butter** or **mignonette lettuce**. Sprinkle with 2 teaspoons lightly toasted **sesame seeds**.

tahini / *pantry*

201

tomatoes are also used in recipes on pages...
13, 25, 55, 81, 89, 95, 99, 103, 111, 117, 119, 131, 137, 143, 177, 181, 193, 207 and 215.

tomatoes

three ways with

ginger tomato fish stew with coriander rice

Cook 400 g (14 oz/2 cups) long-grain rice in boiling water for 10–12 minutes. Drain well and stir through 1 handful coriander (cilantro) leaves, finely chopped. Meanwhile, put 1 chopped onion, 2 garlic cloves and 1 tablespoon grated ginger in a food processor and whiz to a smooth paste. Heat a splash of vegetable oil in a saucepan and cook the paste for 5 minutes over a gentle heat until fragrant. Add 400 g (14 oz) tinned chopped tomatoes, 125 ml (4 fl oz/1/2 cup) water and boil for 5 minutes. Add 2 cubed white fish fillets, stir once and cover. Cook over a gentle heat for 10 minutes. Season well with sea salt and black pepper and serve with the coriander rice.

lamb and rosemary ragout

Cook 1 chopped onion, 1 chopped garlic clove and 1 tablespoon rosemary needles in a splash of olive oil for a few minutes, so the onion gently softens in the oil. Add 500 g (1 lb 2 oz) cubed lamb shoulder, 400 g (14 oz) tinned chopped tomatoes and 250 ml (9 fl oz/1 cup) each red wine and water. Bring to the boil and simmer on a gentle heat for 1 1/2 hours, stirring often, until the lamb is really tender. Season well and serve with potato mash, risoni or soft polenta.

roasted tomato pasta sauce

Have your oven hot and ready at 180°C (350°F/Gas 4). Put 800 g (1 lb 12 oz) tinned tomatoes in a baking tray with 1 quartered onion, 2 chopped garlic cloves and a good pinch of sea salt and sugar. If you want, add a pinch of bicarbonate of soda (baking soda) to help neutralize the sometimes acidic taste of tinned tomatoes. Cook in the oven for 1 hour. Whiz the mixture in a food processor with a handful of basil. Toss through your favourite pasta and serve with lots of grated parmesan. Pouring (whipping) cream can be added to make soup, and the sauce can be used as a base for pizzas.

tomato passata is also used in recipes on pages...
37, 39, 71 and 209.

tomato passata

creamy tomato and basil soup

Cook 1 chopped **garlic clove** and 1 chopped **onion** in 20 g (³/4 oz) sizzling **butter** for 3–4 minutes, to soften the onions. Add 750 ml (26 fl oz/3 cups) **tomato passata (puréed tomatoes)** and a handful of **basil** to the pan. Bring to the boil and simmer for a couple of minutes. Pour into a food processor and blend until smooth. Return to the saucepan and stir through 125 ml (4 fl oz/¹/2 cup) **thickened (whipping) cream** and season well with **salt** and **black pepper**. Serve with **toast** sprinkled with **parmesan** and grilled until golden.

pappardelle with anchovies and tomato cream sauce

Cook 400 g (14 oz) **pappardelle** in boiling water for 8–10 minutes. Drain well and return to the warm saucepan. Meanwhile, heat a few splashes of good **fruity olive oil** in a saucepan with 3–4 **anchovy fillets** and sizzle the anchovies over a gentle heat so they break up and flavour the oil. Add 3 chopped **garlic cloves** and stir-fry for a minute (don't burn it) and add 250 ml (9 fl oz/1 cup) **tomato passata (puréed tomatoes)**. Simmer for 10 minutes and add 3 tablespoons **pouring (whipping) cream**. Toss through the pasta and top with grated **parmesan**.

poppy seed and lime chicken curry

Heat a splash of **vegetable oil** in a frying pan and cook 4 **chicken thigh fillets**, cut into large bite-sized pieces, for 4–5 minutes until golden. Remove from the pan. Add 1 chopped **onion**, 8–10 **curry leaves**, 1 tablespoon **poppy seeds** and a good grinding of **black pepper** to the pan and stir-fry for 2–3 minutes, so the onion sizzles and browns in the hot oil. Add 2 tablespoons **mild Indian curry paste**, stir-fry for 2–3 minutes then return the chicken to the pan with 500 ml (17 fl oz/2 cups) **tomato passata (puréed tomatoes)** and 250 ml (9 fl oz/1 cup) water. Bring to the boil, then reduce the heat to a rapid simmer for 30 minutes. Stir through 3 tablespoons **lime juice** and a handful of roughly chopped **coriander (cilantro) leaves**.

tuna is also used in recipes on pages...
19, 23, 105 and 191.

tuna

three ways with

tuna and eggplant rigatoni

Cook 400 g (14 oz) **rigatoni** in boiling water for 8–10 minutes. Drain and return to the pan. Meanwhile, heat a few tablespoons of **olive oil** in a frying pan and sizzle 1 **small eggplant (aubergine)**, chopped into 2 cm (³/4 inch) cubes, in the hot oil until golden. Add ¹/2 teaspoon **dried oregano**, 400 g (14 oz) tinned **chopped tomatoes** and 125 ml (4 fl oz/ ¹/2 cup) water and simmer rapidly for 8–10 minutes. Stir through 370 g (13 oz) tinned **tuna**, drained of excess oil, and a handful of **black olives**. Stir through to warm but don't break up the tuna too much. Add to the pasta, toss together and serve.

tapas tuna salad

Cook 6 thickly sliced **small boiling potatoes** (try nicola) in boiling water for 8–10 minutes. Add 175 g (6 oz) **asparagus**, cut in half and with woody ends trimmed, to the water for 1 minute. Rinse the vegetables under cold water and drain well. Toss the potato and asparagus in a bowl with 450 g (1 lb) tinned **tuna**, drained of excess oil, a handful of **green olives**, ¹/2 teaspoon **chilli flakes**, 1 sliced **small red onion** and 2 tablespoons good **olive oil**. Sprinkle over ¹/2 teaspoon **smoked paprika** and serve with some **lemon wedges** on the side.

tuna fattoush

Have your oven hot and ready at 220°C (425°F/Gas 7). Tear up 2 pieces of **lavash** (or other unleavened bread) into bite-sized pieces, place on a tray and into the oven for 10 minutes, turning once, until crispy. Gently toss together 2 chopped **Lebanese (short) cucumbers**, 2 chopped ripe and tasty **tomatoes**, 4 sliced **spring onions (scallions)**, 1 handful each **black olives** and **mint**, 2 tablespoons **olive oil** and 1 tablespoon **red wine vinegar**. Add the toasted bread and 375 g (13 oz) tinned **tuna**, drained of excess oil, and gently toss (don't break up the tuna too much). Grind some **black pepper** over the top or, if you have some in your pantry, sprinkle over 2 teaspoons **sumac** instead.

turkish bread

three ways with

cheat's pizza

Have your oven hot and ready at 220°C (425°F/Gas 7). Cut a 20 cm (8 inch) piece of Turkish (pide/flat) bread in half to give two thinner pieces and spread with 3 tablespoons **tomato passata (puréed tomatoes)** and 2 tablespoons **basil pesto** over each. Top each with a handful of sliced **leg ham**, 6 small pitted **black olives**, 1 sliced **large bocconcini ball (fresh baby mozzarella)**, a sprinkling of **dried oregano** and the slightest drizzle of **olive oil**. Put on a baking tray and blast in the oven for 10 minutes.

toasty spiced fingers

Lightly toast 2 tablespoons **sesame seeds** in a frying pan until golden and aromatic, shaking the pan all the time so they cook evenly. Add 2 teaspoons **dried oregano**, 2 teaspoons chopped **thyme**, 2 teaspoons **sumac** and 1 teaspoon **sea salt**. Shake the pan for a minute over a high heat and pour the spice mix into a bowl to cool. Cover until ready to use. Have your oven hot and ready at 220°C (425°F/Gas 7). Cut a 20 cm (8 inch) piece of Turkish (pide/flat) bread in half to give two thinner pieces, brush 3 tablespoons **olive oil** evenly over the bread and sprinkle 1 tablespoon of the spice mixture over each piece. Pop on a baking tray and into the oven for 5 minutes. Remove and allow to cool a bit before cutting into 3 cm (1¼ inch) slices to have dipped into **soft-boiled eggs** or on a Middle Eastern platter.

turkish fig pudding

Have your oven hot and ready at 200°C (400°F/Gas 6). Grease a 1–1.5 litre (35–52 fl oz/4–6 cup) ovenproof dish. Cut a 10 cm (4 inch) wide piece of Turkish (pide/flat) bread in half to give two thinner pieces and roughly tear into smaller bite-sized pieces. Combine 40 g (1½ oz) softened **butter** and 3 tablespoons **fig jam** in a bowl, spread over the pieces of bread and arrange them in the bottom of the dish. Combine 250 ml (9 fl oz/ 1 cup) **pouring (whipping) cream**, 250 ml (9 fl oz/1 cup) **milk**, 2 **eggs** and 115 g (4 oz/½ cup) **caster (superfine) sugar** in a bowl (if you have any **rosewater**, add 1 teaspoon here for a truly Turkish experience), pour over the bread and cook in the oven for 30 minutes.

udon noodles

three ways with

ginger teriyaki eggplant

Cook 300 g (10 1/2 oz) **dried udon noodles** in boiling water for 4–5 minutes and drain well. Combine 2 tablespoons **soy sauce** in a bowl with 250 ml (9 fl oz/ 1 cup) **chicken stock**, 2 teaspoons finely grated **ginger**, 1 crushed **garlic clove**, 1 teaspoon **sugar** and 1 teaspoon **sesame oil**. Slice an **eggplant (aubergine)** into 8 rounds. Heat 3 tablespoons **vegetable oil** in a hot wok or frying pan and cook the eggplant slices for 2 minutes each side. Remove the eggplant and drain all the oil from the wok. Pour in the sauce mixture. Bring to the boil then reduce the heat to a simmer for 2 minutes. Return the eggplant to the pan, tossing to coat in the sauce and cook for a further 2–3 minutes, until the sauce is thick and glossy. Add the noodles, gently tossing to coat in the eggplant and sauce. Serve sprinkled with 2 finely shredded **spring onions (scallions)** and **rice**.

duck and udon soup

Bring 1 litre (35 fl oz/4 cups) **chicken stock** to the boil. Finely shred the meat and skin of half a **Chinese barbecued duck**. Put the duck bones (this is where all the Chinese spice flavours hide) into the saucepan and cook for 5 minutes in the chicken stock. Strain, discard the bones, and return the stock to the pan. Now add the duck meat to the pan with 100 g (3 1/2 oz) **shiitake mushrooms**, stems cut off, 2 handfuls chopped **Chinese greens** (try Chinese broccoli) and a few splashes of **soy sauce**. Meanwhile, cook 300 g (10 1/2 oz) **dried udon noodles** in boiling water for 3–4 minutes. Drain and add to the duck soup. Serve with a drizzle of **sesame oil**.

five-spice chicken with buttered udon

Quarter 4 **chicken thigh fillets** and toss around in a bowl with 1 teaspoon **five-spice**, 2 teaspoons grated **ginger** and 2 tablespoons **soy sauce**. Set aside for 30 minutes. Heat a frying pan to high and add a splash of **cooking oil**. Add the chicken, shaking off and reserving any excess marinade, and stir-fry for a few minutes until well browned. Add the marinade to the pan with 250 ml (9 fl oz/1 cup) **chicken stock**. Bring to the boil, reduce the heat and simmer for 10 minutes. Cook 300 g (10 1/2 oz) **dried udon noodles** in boiling water for 4–5 minutes. Add the noodles to the pan with 40 g (1 1/2 oz) **butter**, toss around to evenly combine then serve.

walnuts are also used in recipes on pages...
21, 35 and 41.

walnuts

three ways with

walnut, goat's cheese and bean salad

Cook 4 large handfuls **mixed beans** (try both green and yellow varieties) in boiling water for 2 minutes. Drain well. Heat a good few splashes of **olive oil** in a frying pan and cook 1 chopped **garlic clove** for a few seconds to flavour the oil. Add the beans to the pan and cook for a few minutes, to coat in the garlicky oil then add 2 tablespoons **red wine vinegar** to the pan. Stir around for a minute and add 1 small handful **flat-leaf (Italian) parsley**, chopped, and 60 g (2 1/4 oz/ 1/2 cup) crumbled **goat's cheese** to the pan with a good grinding of **black pepper**. Stir for a minute, until the goat's cheese is just starting to melt and serve with 60 g (2 1/4 oz/ 1/2 cup) lightly toasted chopped **walnuts** sprinkled over.

waldorf salad thai-style

Put the shredded meat from a **barbecued chicken** in a bowl with 1 large handful **coriander (cilantro) leaves and stems**, roughly chopped, 2 **green apples**, cut into thin strips, 2 finely sliced **celery stalks** and 100 g (3 1/2 oz/1 cup) lightly toasted **walnuts**. Combine 250 g (9 oz/1 cup) **mayonnaise** with 2 tablespoons **fish sauce** and 1 tablespoon **lime juice** and add to the salad. Toss to evenly combine all the ingredients.

caramel walnut tart

Have your oven hot and ready at 220°C (425°F/Gas 7). Fold the edges of a sheet of **puff pastry** over to make a 1 cm (1/2 in) border. Place on a baking tray and cook in the oven for 10 minutes. Meanwhile, combine 2 tablespoons **thick (double/heavy) cream**, 40 g (1 1/2 oz) **butter**, 3 tablespoons **soft brown sugar** and 3 tablespoons **honey** in a saucepan and cook over a gentle heat, stirring constantly, until the mixture looks like smooth caramel. Add 250 g (9 oz/2 cups) **walnuts** and stir to coat the walnuts in the caramel. Spoon evenly over the tart and cook in the oven for a further 10 minutes. Serve warm with **ice cream**.

white vinegar is also used in a recipe on page...
57.

white vinegar

three ways with

easy hollandaise

Combine 3 **egg yolks** and 1 tablespoon **white vinegar** (but even better if you have white wine vinegar) in a food processor for a few seconds. Heat 200 g (7 oz) **butter** in a saucepan until it is bubbling hot, being careful not to burn it. With the motor running, slowly pour the hot butter into the food processor in a steady stream. Remove to a bowl and set aside for 10 minutes to thicken slightly. Season well and serve over **poached eggs** or **salmon fillets**, with **chips (fries)** or **fillet steak**.

corn chips with jalapeño salsa

Roughly chop 4 firm **tomatoes** and put in a food processor with 1 chopped **garlic clove**, 1 chopped **small red onion**, 2 tablespoons **pickled jalapeño chillies** and a tablespoon of the **brine** from the jar, 2 tablespoons **white vinegar** and a good pinch of **salt, black pepper** and **sugar**. Pulse to make a thick, chunky sauce and put in a bowl. Stir through 2 handfuls **coriander (cilantro) leaves**, roughly chopped, and enjoy with warm and crispy **corn chips**.

south indian hot and sour prawn curry

Toss 16 peeled and deveined **raw large prawns (shrimp)**, tails on, in a bowl with 2 tablespoons **mild Indian curry paste** (try madras or balti) so the prawns are evenly coated in the paste. Heat a few splashes of **light olive oil** in a frying pan and stir-fry the prawns for 2–3 minutes over a medium heat. Remove the prawns. Add a little more **oil** to the pan and stir-fry 1 sliced **onion** and 2 chopped **garlic cloves** for 2–3 minutes over a gentle heat. Add 400 g (14 oz) tinned **chopped tomatoes**, stir to combine and boil for 5 minutes, to thicken a little. Return the prawns to the pan with 2 tablespoons **white vinegar** and cook for another minute. Stir through 1 large handful **coriander (cilantro) leaves**, chopped, and serve with **basmati rice** and some warm **naan bread**.

white vinegar / pantry

recipe index

a

affogato, adults only 69
almonds
    almond and parsley pesto 87
    buttery chicken and almond curry 87
    stir-fried chicken with almonds 87
anchovies
    anchovy and caper mayonnaise 43
    chilli tomato risoni 89
    jansson's temptation 89
    olive, tomato and anchovy tart 89
    pappardelle with anchovies and
        tomato cream sauce 205
apples
    apple crumble 163
    hot apple danish 77
apricots
    moroccan chicken with apricots 123
    smoked chicken, apricot and
        feta salad 123
    tipsy apricots with pistachio yoghurt and
        honey 123
artichokes
    artichoke, orange and feta salad 31
    artichoke pesto 91
    artichoke, salami and olive tortilla 99
    broad bean, artichoke and marinated
        feta salad 63
    creamy artichoke soup 91
    fusilli with feta, artichoke and cherry
        tomato sauce 91
asian coleslaw 43
asparagus
    asparagus and goat's cheese tart 79
    asparagus and mozzarella omelette 45
    chilli parmesan asparagus 47
    tapas tuna salad 207
aubergine *see* eggplant

avocado
    avocado and crispy prosciutto salad 183
    broad bean and avocado guacamole 63

b

baked beans, mexican 137
balsamic glazed t-bone 93
bananas, banoffee meringue pie 157
bang bang chicken salad 201
banoffee meringue pie 157
barbecued duck rice salad 199
barbecued haloumi in vine leaves 83
bean thread noodles
    chicken noodle hotpot 95
    spicy fish soup 95
    spicy pork noodles 95
beans
    black bean pork and broccoli hotpot 185
    lentil and bean curry 177
    mexican baked beans 137
    smoky sausage and bean casserole 103
    spicy thai lamb cutlets with beans and
        basil 179
    spicy thai prawns with beans and basil 75
    walnut, goat's cheese and bean salad 213
    see also broad beans; butterbeans;
        cannellini beans; kidney beans
beef
    balsamic glazed t-bone 93
    chilli bean burrito 99
    curried beef shepherd's pie 119
    red wine and beef casserole 181
    slow braised gingered beef 165
    spicy peanut beef with fragrant
        thai basil 171
    steak, onion and ale casserole 17
    stir-fried, with broccolini and
        oyster sauce 165

berries
    blueberry sour cream pudding 61
    creamy oat and raspberry pudding 163
    maple berry compote 61
    messy berry pav 61
    raspberry and croissant puddings 141
    strawberry and passionfruit trifle 151
black bean pork and broccoli hotpot 185
blue cheese
    blue cheese and broad bean risotto 21
    blue cheese and peach salad 21
    blue cheese and walnut pizza with pear
        and rocket salad 21
blueberry sour cream pudding 61
bread, golden cornbread 65
bread and butter pudding, italian 167
bread puddings, ginger and
    marmalade 155
broad beans
    blue cheese and broad bean risotto 21
    broad bean, artichoke and marinated
        feta salad 63
    broad bean and avocado guacamole 63
    creamy broad bean mash 63
bruschetta pizza with tomato, anchovy and
    basil 73
buckwheat noodles
    buckwheat noodle salad with grilled lamb,
        mint and feta 97
    japanese mushroom and leek broth 97
    with smoked chicken, lime and
        sesame 97
burrito, chilli bean 99
butterbeans
    creamy, garlicky bean dip 101
    tapas 101
    Tuscan 101
buttery chicken and almond curry 87

C

cajun corn chowder 109
cannellini beans
    really chunky white bean and pancetta
        soup 103
    smoky sausage and bean casserole 103
    white bean and tuna salad 103
caper and herb sauce 105
caponata, herbed 183
capsicum
    corn, capsicum and coriander stir-fry 65
    nutty red pesto 47
caramel
    banoffee meringue pie 157
    caramel chicken 127
    caramel walnut tart 213
    sweet pork larb in baby cos 127
cashews
    cashew and dill pesto 107
    cashew tabouleh in crisp lettuce 107
    grilled zucchini, cashew and feta salad 107
casseroles
    chicken cacciatore 55
    red wine and beef 181
    slow braised gingered beef 165
    slow-cooked miso and ginger
        pork belly 159
    smoky sausage and beans 103
    steak, onion and ale 17
    tuna 23
    see also hotpot; stews
cauliflower
    cauliflower in spiced yoghurt 57
    fried, with lemon tahini 201
    really cheesy cauliflower 23
cheat's chinese short soup 109
cheat's pizza 209
cheat's tom yum soup 75
cheese
    baked macaroni cheese with ham 37
    barbecued haloumi in vine leaves 83
    ham, mushroom and mozzarella pizza 37
    mascarpone and gorgonzola linguine 41
    provençal tomato and cheese tart 79
    puff pastry with tomato, haloumi and
        mint salad 77
    really cheesy cauliflower 23
    spinach and cheese curry 139
    tomato gratin 175
    tuna casserole 23
    see also blue cheese; cream cheese; feta;
        goat's cheese; mascarpone;
        parmesan; ricotta
chicken
    bang bang chicken salad 201
    buttery chicken and almond curry 87
    caramel chicken 127

chicken (continued)
    chicken and bacon goulash 53
    chicken biryani 147
    chicken cacciatore 55
    chicken curry 119
    chicken and leek pasta 23
    chicken mayonnaise salad 43
    chicken noodle hotpot 95
    chicken noodle soup 109
    chicken and vegetable pot pie 15
    chicken with spiced buttered lentils 177
    chinatown chicken and watercress
        salad 15
    coconut and makrut leaf chicken
        curry 121
    curry roast chicken 139
    drunken chicken 185
    dry, spicy peanut chicken curry 169
    five spice chicken with buttered udon 211
    ginger teriyaki chicken 195
    gunpowder chicken 169
    herbed chicken schnitzel 175
    moroccan chicken with apricots 123
    poppy seed and lime chicken curry 205
    roasted chicken with green olives,
        balsamic and capers 35
    spicy chicken and pine nut san choy
        bau 173
    spicy lime and peanut chicken 129
    spicy red chicken 179
    spicy sesame chicken salad 189
    stir-fried chicken with almonds 87
    sweet soy chicken wings 185
    tex-mex chicken salad 15
chickpeas
    chickpea sesame dip 111
    chickpea, smoky chorizo and bread
        salad 111
    spinach and chickpea curry 81
chilli
    barbecued duck rice salad 199
    chargrilled chilli prawns 199
    chilli bean burrito 99
    chilli parmesan asparagus 47
    chilli prawn linguine 75
    chilli pumpkin rigatoni 193
    chilli tomato risoni 89
    eggplant in chilli hoisin 133
    herb and chilli ricotta 49
    orange and chilli ribs 155
    pasta with chilli crumbs 197
    shell pasta with chilli, pine nuts and
        broccolini 173
    silky fried tofu with chilli pepper and
        lemon 51
    sticky chilli lime ribs 199
chinatown chicken and watercress salad 15

chinatown mushroom and tofu stir-fry 33
chinese barbecue pork 133
chinese cabbage
    asian coleslaw 43
    stir-fried mushrooms with chinese
        cabbage 125
chocolate
    chocolate pudding 113
    chocolate sauce 113
    drunken chocolate ice cream meringues 157
    over the top chocolate mousse 113
chorizo
    chickpea, smoky chorizo and bread
        salad 111
    chorizo and seafood gumbo 25
    lentil, chorizo and goat's cheese salad 131
    paprika risoni hotpot 25
    spanish minestrone 25
    sweet and sour tapas chorizo 17
coconut
    coconut and curry leaf rice 121
    coconut and makrut leaf chicken curry 121
    coconut, maple and pecan granola 163
    coconut prawns 121
coleslaw, asian 43
corn
    cajun corn chowder 109
    corn, capsicum and coriander stir-fry 65
    corn chips with jalapeño salsa 215
    corn fritters 65
    golden cornbread 65
couscous
    honey pumpkin couscous salad 117
    roast pumpkin, tahini and couscous
        salad 201
    smoky spiced couscous 117
cream cheese
    cream cheese and cherry danish 27
    creamy potato and leek soup 27
    fettucine boscaiola 27
creamy artichoke soup 91
creamy broad bean mash 63
creamy, garlicky bean dip 101
creamy potato and leek soup 27
creamy scrambled eggs with dill 53
creamy spinach and leek soup 81
croque madame 37
curry
    buttery chicken and almond 87
    chicken 119
    chicken biryani 147
    coconut and makrut leaf chicken 121
    crispy skinned fish in jungle curry 129
    curried beef shepherd's pie 119
    curry roast chicken 139
    dry, spicy peanut chicken 169
    easy prawn 115

curry (*continued*)
    fruity duck 179
    green curry with salmon and aromatic
        herbs 129
    indian kidney bean 143
    lentil and bean 177
    madras rack of lamb 139
    massaman curry 115
    pea curry 71
    poppy seed and lime chicken 205
    potato and tomato 115
    south indian hot and sour prawn 215
    spicy lime and peanut chicken 129
    spicy red chicken 179
    spicy thai lamb cutlets with beans and
        basil 179
    spinach and cheese 139
    spinach and chickpea 81
custard, maple 153

d

desserts
    apple crumble 163
    baked vanilla rice pudding 191
    banoffee meringue pie 157
    blueberry sour cream pudding 61
    caramel walnut tart 213
    chocolate pudding 113
    creamy oat and raspberry pudding 163
    drunken chocolate ice cream meringues 157
    ginger and marmalade bread puddings 155
    hot jam and coconut tarts 141
    italian bread and butter pudding 167
    jam cake 141
    maple pears 153
    messy berry pav 61
    over the top chocolate mousse 113
    plum bruschetta 167
    raspberry and croissant puddings 141
    red wine and vanilla figs 181
    tipsy apricots with pistachio yoghurt
        and honey 123
    tiramisu 151
    tropical pav 157
    turkish fig pudding 209
    vanilla peaches 55
    see also ice cream
dips
    broad bean and avocado guacamole 63
    chickpea sesame 111
    creamy, garlicky bean 101
    smoky eggplant, cumin and mint dip 57
duck
    barbecued duck rice salad 199
    duck and udon soup 211
    fruity duck curry 179
    star anise and orange duck 155

e

egg and bacon pie 13
egg noodles
    cold tossed noodle salad 29
    a short long soup 29
    yum cha noodles 29
eggplant
    eggplant in chilli hoisin 133
    ginger teriyaki eggplant 211
    herbed caponata 183
    rigatoni with pea, eggplant and mint
        sauce 71
    smoky eggplant, cumin and mint dip 57
    sweet and sour herbed eggplant salad 127
    tuna and eggplant rigatoni 207
eggs
    asparagus and mozzarella omelette 45
    creamy scrambled eggs with dill 53
    egg and bacon pie 13
    ham and egg fried rice 147
    panettone french toast 167
    salmon omelette 187
    tofu and zucchini omelette 33
    warm spinach, egg and bacon salad 13
espresso mousse 41

f

feta
    artichoke, orange and feta salad 31
    broad bean, artichoke and marinated
        feta salad 63
    creamy feta salad dressing 31
    fusilli with feta, artichoke and cherry
        tomato sauce 91
    grilled zucchini, cashew and feta salad 107
    lamb and feta filo parcels 67
    mushroom and feta pie 67
    prawns with feta 31
    roasted lamb rack with marinated feta and
        lentils 131
    roasted vegetable, feta and mint
        quesadilla 99
    smoked chicken, apricot and feta salad 123
fettucine boscaiola 27
figs
    red wine and vanilla figs 181
    turkish fig pudding 209
filo
    lamb and feta filo parcels 67
    mushroom and feta pie 67
    salmon dill pie 67
fish
    crispy skinned fish in jungle curry 129
    ginger tomato fish stew with coriander
        rice 203
    lime pickle, coriander and soy swordfish 145
    seafood and couscous stew 117

fish (*continued*)
    spaghetti with fried sardines, parsley and
        lemon 149
    spicy fish soup 95
    steamed vine leaf fish with dill and
        lemon 83
    see also salmon; seafood
five spice maple glazed pork 153
french toast, panettone 167
fried rice
    ham and egg 147
    prawn, leek and pine nut 147
fruity duck curry 179
fusilli with feta, artichoke and cherry tomato
    sauce 91

g

ginger
    ginger and marmalade bread puddings 155
    ginger teriyaki chicken 195
    ginger teriyaki eggplant 211
    ginger tomato fish stew with coriander
        rice 203
    slow braised gingered beef 165
    slow-cooked miso and ginger pork belly 159
goat's cheese
    asparagus and goat's cheese tart 79
    baked mushrooms and goat's cheese in
        vine leaves 83
    lentil, chorizo and goat's cheese salad 131
    walnut, goat's cheese and bean salad 213
golden cornbread 65
goulash, chicken and bacon 53
grandma's tofu and pork hotpot 51
granola, coconut, maple and pecan 163
green curry with salmon and aromatic
    herbs 129
guacamole, broad bean and avocado 63

h

haloumi
    barbecued in vine leaves 83
    puff pastry with tomato, haloumi and
        mint salad 77
ham
    baked macaroni cheese with ham 37
    croque madame 37
    ham and egg fried rice 147
    ham, mushroom and mozzarella pizza 37
herb and chilli ricotta 49
herbed caponata 183
herbed chicken schnitzel 175
herby olive sauce 19
hollandaise sauce, easy 215
honey
    honey prawns 135
    honey pumpkin couscous 117

honey (*continued*)
   honey-and-spice lamb cutlets 135
   tofu with honey and black pepper 135
hot apple danish 77
hot jam and coconut tarts 141
hotpot
   black bean pork and broccoli 185
   chicken noodle 95
   grandma's tofu and pork 51
   paprika risoni 25
   slow braised lamb shank and
      vegetable 17
   see also casseroles
hot and sour mushroom soup 125

i

ice cream
   adults only affogato 69
   drunken chocolate ice cream
      meringues 157
   tutti-frutti 69
indian kidney bean curry 143
italian bread and butter pudding 167
italian chickpea soup 111

j

jam
   hot jam and coconut tarts 141
   jam cake 141
jansson's temptation 89
japanese mushroom and leek
   broth 97

k

kidney beans
   chilli bean burrito 99
   indian kidney bean curry 143
   smoky bean nachos 143
   spiced potato and bean salad 143
korean sesame barbecue marinade 189

l

lamb
   buckwheat noodle salad with grilled lamb,
      mint and feta 97
   honey-and-spice lamb cutlets 135
   lamb and feta filo parcels 67
   lamb and rosemary ragout 203
   lamb wellington 77
   madras rack of lamb 139
   massaman curry 115
   miso and lemon thyme crumbed lamb
      fillets 159
   mongolian lamb cutlets 133
   parmesan and herb crumbed lamb
      cutlets 197
   persian lamb pizza 173

lamb (*continued*)
   roasted lamb rack with marinated feta and
      lentils 131
   savoury lamb pie 79
   slow braised lamb shank and vegetable
      hotpot 17
   slow-cooked lamb shank with lentils 131
   spicy thai lamb cutlets with beans and
      basil 179
lasagne
   hand-cut pasta with nutty sage butter 39
   tomato and spinach lasagne 39
   zucchini and ricotta cannelloni 39
leeks
   chicken and leek pasta 23
   creamy potato and leek soup 27
   creamy spinach and leek soup 81
   japanese mushroom and leek broth 97
   prawn, leek and pine nut fried rice 147
   silky leek and miso risotto 159
lentils
   chicken with spiced buttered lentils 177
   lentil and bean curry 177
   lentil, chorizo and goat's cheese salad 131
   mediterranean lentil soup 177
   roasted lamb rack with marinated feta and
      lentils 131
   slow-cooked lamb shank with lentils 131
   spiced tomato and lentil soup 119
lime pickle
   lime pickle, coriander and soy swordfish 145
   pumpkin with lime pickle dressing 145
   zesty lime pickle rice 145
linguine
   chilli prawn 75
   mascarpone and gorgonzola 41
   smoked chicken 149

m

macaroni cheese, baked, with ham 37
madras rack of lamb 139
maple syrup
   coconut, maple and pecan granola 163
   five spice maple glazed pork 153
   maple berry compote 61
   maple custard 153
   maple pears 153
   orange maple mascarpone 41
marinade, korean sesame barbecue 189
mascarpone
   espresso mousse 41
   mascarpone and gorgonzola linguine 41
   orange maple mascarpone 41
massaman curry 115
mayonnaise
   anchovy and caper 43
   tabasco 137

mediterranean lentil soup 177
meringue
   banoffee meringue pie 157
   drunken chocolate ice cream meringues 157
   messy berry pav 61
   strawberry meringue parfait 69
   tropical pav 157
mexican baked beans 137
miso and lemon thyme crumbed lamb
   fillets 159
mongolian lamb cutlets 133
moroccan chicken with apricots 123
mousse
   espresso 41
   over the top chocolate 113
mozzarella
   asparagus and mozzarella omelette 45
   ham, mushroom and mozzarella pizza 37
   mozzarella and prosciutto tortilla 45
   tomato, pesto and mozzarella pizza 45
mushrooms
   baked with goat's cheese in vine leaves 83
   chinatown mushroom and tofu stir-fry 33
   ham, mushroom and mozzarella pizza 37
   hot and sour mushroom soup 125
   japanese mushroom and leek broth 97
   mushroom and feta pie 67
   san choy bau of pork, mushroom and
      water chestnut 165
   simmered mushrooms with tofu 125
   stir-fried mushrooms with chinese
      cabbage 125
mustard
   mustard and herb crumbed veal cutlets 161
   potato salad with mustard basil
      dressing 161
   tomato, basil and mustard tart 161

n

niçoise rice salad 191
noodles
   chicken noodle soup 109
   stir-fried vegetables with peanut
      noodles 171
   see also bean thread noodles; buckwheat
      noodles; egg noodles; udon noodles
nutty red pesto 47

o

oats
   apple crumble 163
   coconut, maple and pecan granola 163
   creamy oat and raspberry pudding 163
octopus, slow-cooked in red wine, tomato
   and olive sauce 181
olives
   artichoke, salami and olive tortilla 99

olives (*continued*)
    herby olive sauce 19
    olive and roasted cherry tomato
        pasta sauce 19
    olive, tomato and anchovy tart 89
    orange and olive salad 35
    penne with olives, tuna and chilli
        herbs 19
    roasted chicken with green olives,
        balsamic and capers 35
    turkish olive and walnut salad 35
omelettes
    asparagus and mozzarella 45
    salmon 187
    tofu and zucchini 33
oranges
    artichoke, orange and feta salad 31
    orange and chilli ribs 155
    orange maple mascarpone 41
    orange and olive salad 35
    star anise and orange duck 155

p

panettone
    italian bread and butter pudding 167
    panettone french toast 167
    plum bruschetta 167
paprika risoni hotpot 25
parmesan
    chilli parmesan asparagus 47
    nutty red pesto 47
    parmesan and garlic spaghetti 47
    parmesan and herb crumbed lamb
        cutlets 197
pappardelle with anchovies and tomato
    cream sauce 205
pasta
    baked macaroni cheese with ham 37
    fettucine boscaiola 27
    fusilli with feta, artichoke and cherry
        tomato sauce 91
    pappardelle with anchovies and tomato
        cream sauce 205
    pasta with chilli crumbs 197
    ricotta, tomato and basil pasta salad 49
    rigatoni with pea, eggplant and mint
        sauce 71
    sicilian chicken and pine nut pasta
        salad 183
    springtime minestrone 193
    tagliatelle with tuna and lemony
        capers 105
    tuna and eggplant rigatoni 207
    see also lasagne; linguine; penne; risoni;
        shell pasta; spaghetti
pasta sauces
    the easiest spaghetti sauce 149

pasta sauces (*continued*)
    olive and roasted cherry tomato 19
    ricotta and winter greens 49
    roasted tomato 203
pastry; *see* filo; puff pastry; shortcrust pastry
peaches
    blue cheese and peach salad 21
    vanilla peaches 55
peanuts
    dry, spicy peanut chicken curry 169
    gunpowder chicken 169
    satay sauce 171
    spicy lime and peanut chicken 129
    spicy peanut beef with fragrant thai
        basil 171
    stir-fried vegetables with peanut
        noodles 171
    thai peanut pesto 169
pears, maple pears 153
peas
    pea curry 71
    pea soup with crispy prosciutto and
        ricotta toasts 71
    rigatoni with pea, eggplant and mint
        sauce 71
penne
    with bacon, chilli and tomato 13
    with italian sausage, basil and
        pecorino 193
    with olives, tuna and chilli herbs 19
persian lamb pizza 173
pesto
    almond and parsley 87
    artichoke 91
    cashew and dill 107
    nutty red pesto 47
    thai peanut 169
pies
    baked polenta pie 175
    chicken and vegetable pot pie 15
    egg and bacon 13
    mushroom and feta 67
    salmon dill 67
    savoury lamb 79
pine nuts
    persian lamb pizza 173
    shell pasta with chilli, pine nuts and
        broccolini 173
    spicy chicken and pine nut san choy
        bau 173
pizza
    blue cheese and walnut, with pear and
        rocket salad 21
    bruschetta, with tomato, anchovy and
        basil 73
    cheat's pizza 209
    ham, mushroom and mozzarella 37

pizza (*continued*)
    persian lamb 173
    potato, onion and rosemary 73
    spicy spanish 73
    tomato, pesto and mozzarella 45
plum bruschetta 167
polenta
    baked polenta pie 175
    herbed chicken schnitzel 175
    tomato gratin 175
poppy seed and lime chicken curry 205
pork
    black bean pork and broccoli hotpot 185
    chilli bean burrito 99
    chinese barbecue pork 133
    five spice maple glazed pork 153
    grandma's tofu and pork hotpot 51
    orange and chilli ribs 155
    red braised pork fillet 195
    san choy bau of pork, mushroom and
        water chestnut 165
    slow-cooked miso and ginger pork
        belly 159
    spicy pork noodles 95
    sticky chilli lime ribs 199
    sweet pork larb in baby cos 127
potatoes
    creamy potato and leek soup 27
    curried beef shepherd's pie 119
    jansson's temptation 89
    potato, onion and rosemary pizza 73
    potato salad with mustard basil
        dressing 161
    potato and tomato curry 115
    salmon, potato and dill cakes 187
    spiced potato and bean salad 143
    tapas tuna salad 207
    winter mash with bacon and
        sour cream 53
prawns
    chargrilled chilli prawns 199
    chilli prawn linguine 75
    chorizo and seafood gumbo 25
    coconut prawns 121
    crumbed, with plum sauce 197
    easy prawn curry 115
    honey prawns 135
    prawn, leek and pine nut fried rice 147
    prawns with feta 31
    seafood and couscous stew 117
    south indian hot and sour prawn
        curry 215
    spicy thai prawns with beans and basil 75
    tom yum soup 75
puff pastry
    caramel walnut tart 213
    cream cheese and cherry danish 27

puff pastry (*continued*)
  hot apple danish 77
  lamb wellington 77
  with tomato, haloumi and mint salad 77
pumpkin
  chilli pumpkin rigatoni 193
  honey pumpkin couscous salad 117
  pumpkin with lime pickle dressing 145
  roast pumpkin, tahini and couscous
    salad 201

q

quesadilla, roasted vegetable, feta and mint 99

r

raspberry and croissant puddings 141
red wine
  red wine and beef casserole 181
  red wine and vanilla figs 181
  slow-cooked octopus in red wine, tomato
    and olive sauce 181
rice
  baked vanilla rice pudding 191
  barbecued duck rice salad 199
  chicken biryani 147
  coconut and curry leaf rice 121
  ginger tomato fish stew with coriander
    rice 203
  niçoise rice salad 191
  spicy tomato rice 137
  zesty lime pickle rice 145
  see also fried rice; risotto
ricotta
  herb and chilli ricotta 49
  pea soup with crispy prosciutto and
    ricotta toasts 71
  plum bruschetta 167
  ricotta, tomato and basil pasta salad 49
  ricotta and winter green pasta sauce 49
  shell pasta with ricotta and spinach 81
  zucchini and ricotta cannelloni 49
risoni
  chilli tomato 89
  paprika risoni hotpot 25
risotto
  baked tuna and zucchini 191
  blue cheese and broad bean 21
  silky leek and miso 159
  tipsy lemon 55

s

salad dressing, creamy feta 31
salads
  artichoke, orange and feta 31
  avocado and crispy prosciutto 183
  bang bang chicken 201
  barbecued duck rice salad 199

salads (*continued*)
  blue cheese and peach 21
  broad bean, artichoke and marinated
    feta 63
  buckwheat noodles with grilled lamb, mint
    and feta 97
  cashew tabouleh in crisp lettuce 107
  chicken mayonnaise salad 43
  chickpea, smoky chorizo and bread 111
  chinatown chicken and watercress 15
  cold tossed noodle 29
  grilled zucchini, cashew and feta 107
  honey pumpkin couscous 117
  lentil, chorizo and goat's cheese 131
  niçoise rice salad 191
  orange and olive 35
  potato salad with mustard basil dressing 161
  ricotta, tomato and basil pasta 49
  roast pumpkin, tahini and couscous 201
  sicilian chicken and pine nut pasta 183
  smoked chicken, apricot and feta 123
  spiced potato and bean 143
  spicy sesame chicken 189
  sweet and sour herbed eggplant 127
  tapas tuna 207
  tex-mex chicken 15
  turkish cucumber 57
  turkish olive and walnut 35
  waldorf salad thai-style 213
  walnut, goat's cheese and bean 213
  warm spinach, egg and bacon 13
  white bean and tuna 103
salami, artichoke, salami and olive tortilla 99
salmon
  green curry with salmon and aromatic
    herbs 129
  salmon dill pie 67
  salmon omelette 187
  salmon, potato and dill cakes 187
  salmon shepherd's pie 187
san choy bau
  of pork, mushroom and water chestnut 165
  of spicy chicken and pine nuts 173
satay sauce 171
sauces
  caper and herb 105
  chocolate 113
  easy hollandaise 215
  herby olive 19
  satay sauce 171
  see also pasta sauces
sausage
  penne with Italian sausage, basil and
    pecorino 193
  smoky bean nachos 143
  smoky sausage and bean casserole 103
  see also chorizo

seafood
  chorizo and seafood gumbo 25
  seafood and couscous stew 117
  slow-cooked octopus in red wine, tomato
    and olive sauce 181
  see also fish; salmon
sesame seeds
  korean sesame barbecue marinade 189
  sesame-crusted tuna steaks with wasabi
    mayonnaise 189
  spicy sesame chicken salad 189
shell pasta
  chicken and leek 23
  with chilli, pine nuts and broccolini 173
  with ricotta and spinach 81
shepherd's pie
  curried beef 119
  salmon 187
short long soup 29
shortcrust pastry
  asparagus and goat's cheese tart 79
  hot jam and coconut tarts 141
  provençal tomato and cheese tart 79
  savoury lamb pie 79
sicilian chicken and pine nut pasta salad 183
sicilian grape and mascarpone cake 151
smoked chicken
  buckwheat noodles with smoked chicken,
    lime and sesame 97
  sicilian chicken and pine nut pasta
    salad 183
  smoked chicken, apricot and feta
    salad 123
  smoked chicken linguine 149
soups
  cajun corn chowder 109
  cheat's chinese short soup 109
  chicken noodle 109
  creamy artichoke 91
  creamy spinach and leek 81
  creamy tomato and basil 205
  duck and udon 211
  hot and sour mushroom 125
  italian chickpea 111
  japanese mushroom and leek broth 97
  mediterranean lentil 177
  pea soup with crispy prosciutto and
    ricotta toasts 71
  really chunky white bean and pancetta
    soup 103
  a short long soup 29
  spanish minestrone 25
  spiced tomato and lentil 119
  spicy fish 95
  springtime minestrone 193
  tom yum 75
south indian hot and sour prawn curry 215

soy sauce
ginger teriyaki chicken 195
ginger teriyaki eggplant 211
red braised pork fillet 195
soy-simmered vegetables with tofu 195
sweet soy chicken wings 185

spaghetti
with balsamic tomatoes 93
the easiest spaghetti sauce 149
with fried sardines, parsley and lemon 149
parmesan and garlic 47

spanish minestrone 25
spicy fish soup 95
spicy pork noodles 95
spicy sour tofu 93
spicy spanish pizza 73
spicy thai prawns with beans and basil 75
spicy tomato rice 137

spinach
creamy spinach and leek soup 81
shell pasta with ricotta and spinach 81
spinach and cheese curry 139
spinach and chickpea curry 81
tomato and spinach lasagne 39
warm spinach, egg and bacon salad 13

springtime minestrone 193
star anise and orange duck 155
steak, onion and ale casserole 17

stews
chicken and bacon goulash 53
ginger tomato fish stew with coriander rice 203
lamb and rosemary ragout 203
seafood and couscous 117
see also casseroles; hotpot

stir-fries
beef with broccolini and oyster sauce 165
chicken with almonds 87
chinatown mushroom and tofu 33
corn, capsicum and coriander 65
mushrooms with chinese cabbage 125
vegetables with peanut noodles 171

strawberry meringue parfait 69
strawberry and passionfruit trifle 151
sweet and sour herbed eggplant salad 127
sweet and sour tapas chorizo 17

t
tabasco mayonnaise 137
tabouleh, cashew, in crisp lettuce 107
tagliatelle with tuna and lemony capers 105
tapas butterbeans 101
tapas tuna salad 207

tarts
asparagus and goat's cheese 79
caramel walnut 213
olive, tomato and anchovy 89

tarts (continued)
provençal tomato and cheese 79
tomato, basil and mustard 161
upside-down caper and tomato 105

tex-mex chicken salad 15
thai peanut pesto 169
tipsy lemon risotto 55
tiramisu 151
toasty spiced fingers 209

tofu
braised, in ginger, spring onion and oyster sauce 33
chinatown mushroom and tofu stir-fry 33
grandma's tofu and pork hotpot 51
with honey and black pepper 135
silky fried tofu with chilli pepper and lemon 51
simmered mushrooms with tofu 125
soy-simmered vegetables with tofu 195
spicy sour tofu 93
steamed, with ginger and spring onions 51
tofu and zucchini omelette 33

tom yum soup 75

tomatoes
chilli tomato risoni 89
creamy tomato and basil soup 205
ginger tomato fish stew with coriander rice 203
lamb and rosemary ragout 203
olive and roasted cherry tomato pasta sauce 19
pappardelle with anchovies and tomato cream sauce 205
potato and tomato curry 115
provençal tomato and cheese tart 79
puff pastry with tomato, haloumi and mint salad 77
ricotta, tomato and basil pasta salad 49
roasted tomato pasta sauce 203
spaghetti with balsamic tomatoes 93
spiced tomato and lentil soup 119
spicy tomato rice 137
tomato, basil and mustard tart 161
tomato gratin 175
tomato, pesto and mozzarella pizza 45
tomato and spinach lasagne 39
upside-down caper and tomato tart 105

tortilla, mozzarella and prosciutto 45
trifle, strawberry and passionfruit 151

tuna
baked tuna and zucchini risotto 191
penne with olives, tuna and chilli herbs 19
sesame-crusted tuna steaks with wasabi mayonnaise 189
tagliatelle with tuna and lemony capers 105
tapas tuna salad 207
tuna casserole 23

tuna and eggplant rigatoni 207
tuna fattoush 207
white bean and tuna salad 103
Turkish cucumber salad 57
Turkish fig pudding 209
Turkish olive and walnut salad 35
Tuscan butterbeans 101
tutti-frutti ice cream 69

u
udon noodles
duck and udon soup 211
five spice chicken with buttered udon 211
ginger teriyaki eggplant 211

v
vanilla peaches 55
vanilla rice pudding, baked 191
veal, mustard and herb crumbed veal cutlets 161

vegetables
cauliflower in spiced yoghurt 57
creamy broad bean mash 63
fried cauliflower with lemon tahini 201
pea curry 71
pumpkin with lime pickle dressing 145
roasted vegetable, feta and mint quesadilla 99
smoky eggplant, cumin and mint dip 57
soy-simmered vegetables with tofu 195
springtime minestrone 193
stir-fried, with peanut noodles 171
see also mushrooms; salads

w
walnuts
caramel walnut tart 213
waldorf salad thai-style 213
walnut, goat's cheese and bean salad 213

white bean and pancetta soup 103
white bean and tuna salad 103
winter mash with bacon and sour cream 53

xyz
yoghurt
cauliflower in spiced yoghurt 57
smoky eggplant, cumin and mint dip 57
tipsy apricots with pistachio yoghurt and honey 123
turkish cucumber salad 57

yum cha noodles 29

zucchini
baked tuna and zucchini risotto 191
grilled zucchini, cashew and feta salad 107
tofu and zucchini omelette 33
zucchini and ricotta cannelloni 39

thank you

Within a few minutes of discussing this book Kay Scarlett knew we were on to a good thing. Thank you Kay for that confidence and sharing the vision and enthusiasm.

Thank you to Juliet and the rest of the crew at Murdoch Books, a genuinely gorgeous bunch of people. Thanks especially to Viv and Paul for all their hard work. And to Brett, whose photography captured the spirit of this book.

My sister Sue and friend Mikey for coming over and being the most motivated, hands-on helpers/testers/food critics I could wish for. Good one guys and a big hug to both of you.

To BA. Thanks for the laptop rental.

And to Matt. Thanks for being so bloody supportive!

Ross x.

Published in 2007 by Murdoch Books Pty Limited
www.murdochbooks.com.au

Murdoch Books Australia
Pier 8/9
23 Hickson Road
Millers Point NSW 2000
Phone: +61 (0) 2 8220 2000
Fax: +61 (0) 2 8220 2558

Murdoch Books UK Limited
Erico House, 6th Floor North
93/99 Upper Richmond Road
Putney, London SW15 2TG
Phone: +44 (0) 20 8785 5995
Fax: +44 (0) 20 8785 5985

Chief Executive: Juliet Rogers
Publishing Director: Kay Scarlett

Editor: Paul McNally
Design and art direction: Vivien Valk
Photography and styling: Brett Stevens
Props: Jo Briscoe
Production: Maiya Levitch
Colour reproduction: Splitting Image Colour Studio, Melbourne, Australia

National Library of Australia Cataloguing-in-Publication Data:
Dobson, Ross, 1965- . 3 ways with ... : stale bread and 99 other ingredients from your pantry, fridge or freezer. Includes index. ISBN 978 1 74045 884 9. ISBN 1 74045 884 2. 1. Cookery. 2. Quick and easy cookery. I. Title. 641.5

Printed by Midas Printing (Asia) Ltd. in 2007. Printed in China.

Important Those who might be at risk from the effects of salmonella poisoning (the elderly, pregnant women, young children and those suffering from immune deficiency diseases) should consult their doctor with any concerns about eating raw eggs.

Conversion guide You may find cooking times vary depending on the oven you are using. For fan-forced ovens, as a general rule, set the oven temperature to 20°C (35°F) lower than indicated in the recipe. We have used 20 ml (4 teaspoon) tablespoon measures. If you are using a 15 ml (3 teaspoon) tablespoon, for most recipes the difference will not be noticeable. However, for recipes using baking powder, gelatine, bicarbonate of soda (baking soda), small amounts of flour and cornflour (cornstarch), add an extra teaspoon for each tablespoon specified.